serge it!

LARK

An Imprint of Sterling Publishing
387 Park Avenue South
New York, NY 10016

ISBN 978-1-4547-0780-6

Doh, Jenny.
  Serge it! : 24 fun & fresh projects to sew with your serger / Jenny Doh &
    Cynthia Shaffer.
      pages cm
    Includes bibliographical references and index.
    ISBN 978-1-4547-0780-6 (alk. paper)
    1. Serging. 2. Dress accessories. 3. House furnishings. I. Shaffer,
  Cynthia. II. Title.
    TT713.D653 2013
    646.2'044--dc23

                                                    2013033591

Distributed in Canada by Sterling Publishing
c/o Canadian Manda Group, 165 Dufferin Street
Toronto, Ontario, Canada M6K 3H6
Distributed in the United Kingdom by GMC Distribution Services
Castle Place, 166 High Street, Lewes, East Sussex, England BN7 1XU
Distributed in Australia by Capricorn Link (Australia) Pty. Ltd.
P.O. Box 704, Windsor, NSW 2756, Australia

For information about custom editions, special sales, and premium and corporate purchases, please contact Sterling Special Sales at 800-805-5489 or specialsales@sterlingpublishing.com.

Email academic@larkbooks.com for information about desk and examination copies.
The complete policy can be found at larkcrafts.com.

Every effort has been made to ensure that all the information in this book is accurate. However, due to differing conditions, tools, and individual skills, the publisher cannot be responsible for any injuries, losses, and other damages that may result from the use of the information in this book.

Manufactured in China

2 4 6 8 10 9 7 5 3 1

larkcrafts.com

serge it!

24 Fun & Fresh Projects to Sew with Your Serger

jenny doh & cynthia shaffer

LARK

contents

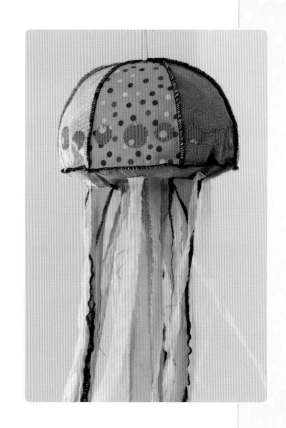

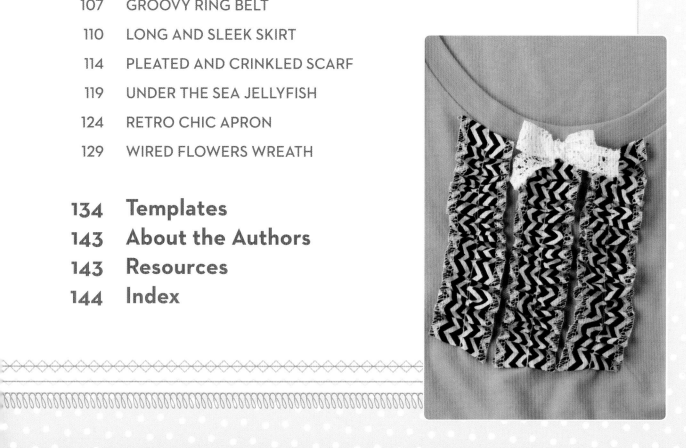

introduction

by Jenny Doh

Years ago when I was a new mom, I took my very first sewing classes from Cynthia Shaffer. It was a thrilling time in my life because I was finally learning the basics of garment construction—something that had been at the top of my creative bucket list for quite some time—on a brand-spanking-new sewing machine. I was eager to sew clothes and quilts for my daughter and son.

After several classes, Cynthia brought her serger into class to show students how our skills could be enhanced with it. It was a machine that looked simultaneously familiar and foreign to me. Four cones of thread all wound onto a machine, with blades that cut the fabric while the threads all worked together: I was intrigued and intimidated at the same time!

But when I really saw what a serger could do, I knew I wanted one. I was impressed with how beautifully seams could be finished, how it could make the coolest decorative edge work, and how garments could be constructed completely with the serger from knits and stretchy fabrics.

So I ended up buying a serger of my own. And though I successfully used it a few times, I admit that it ended up sitting in my closet for many years, mainly because once the sewing classes came to an end, I just couldn't sustain my confidence level for using the serger on my own to the same degree that I could with the sewing machine.

When I talk with other sewers in my life, several have similar stories to tell. It goes like this:

- **Part 1: Learn about the awesome things that sergers can do.**
- **Part 2: Buy a serger.**
- **Part 3: Leave the serger in the closet to collect dust as you overthink and overworry about your ability to successfully use the machine.**

I am excited that Cynthia and I will add Part 4 to your story: Take the serger out of the closet and make the most amazing serged projects in the world.

Did I just say, "the most amazing serged projects in the world?" Why, yes I did! In researching serged projects, we have discovered that there aren't very many projects, let alone *interesting* projects out there. Perhaps this is one of the reasons we serger-owners have been keeping our machines at bay: because of the shortage of inspiring serged projects.

Serge It! is a book that presents instructions with beautiful, clear photographs on how to make 24 fun and easy serged projects. Several of the projects also involve the use of a regular single-needle sewing machine but most of the projects are made from start to finish with just the serger.

Before you dive into the projects, you will want to spend quality time reading the Basics section on pages 8–24, which is filled with valuable information that can help quiet down the intimidation factor and turn up the fun factor when it comes to you and your serger.

Keep in mind that there are different types of sergers made by various manufacturers. Most machines are designed so that you can use three, four, or five threads to create different types of seams and stitches. There are also specialty serger machines that use only two threads, but we will not be working with two-thread machines in this book.

Although there are aesthetic differences from one serger to another, the foundational components are the same. The Basics chapter contains photographs of the parts and pieces from my serger that I bought years ago. Your serger may look slightly different but the main concepts related to blades, needles, loopers, feed dogs, tensions, and differential feeds are universal.

One of the most important things that we recommend as you read the Basics is to do so in conjunction with the owner's manual for your serger. For example, if we show you a photograph of the upper looper tension knob on my serger, you may need to use your owner's manual to find where that knob is located on your machine and what it looks like. Once you find it, the information we provide on how to use it will make sense.

Finally, after you read the Basics chapter *and* your owner's manual, pick out a project in this book and just begin. Because there are so many parts and pieces to understand, you may convince yourself that you're never quite ready to begin. But you know what? You'll be surprised that once you have a general idea of how things work, everything will start coming together as you start a project and learn by doing. Even if you make a few mistakes at first, don't lose heart. Those errors will teach you valuable lessons about your machine. And trust me, once you get the hang of it, you'll have a whole lot of fun!

The Basics

getting to know your serger

When you buy your serger, we highly recommend that you take a class to learn the basics of how to thread the machine and also to familiarize yourself with the owner's manual. These types of classes are typically offered free of charge from stores that sell sewing machines and sergers. If you end up with a serger that is either handed down or purchased online, you can still call local shops and find classes that teach the basics, probably for a nominal fee. These classes are a great investment.

THE PARTS AND PIECES

The serger that was used to make the projects in this book is a four-thread machine (photo 1). Some sergers are older or newer; some use fewer threads, and some use more. Rather than talk about the particulars of every type of serger out there, we will show you close-up photos of the components from the serger used for this book. Even though the design of a certain dial or button may differ from machine to machine, the main components that make up a serger are pretty much the same. You'll most likely be able to find the component on your machine that corresponds to the following:

Serged Stitches

In commercially made garments, the serged seams are usually on the inside, to prevent unraveling. However, most of the projects in this book use serged seams on the right side as decorative elements. Here are the different types of serged stitches that you'll be making for the projects in this book:

- Three-thread 4 mm overlock (photo a)
- Three-thread 6 mm overlock (photo b)
- Four-thread 6 mm overlock (photo c)
- Four-thread 6 mm overlock, color-coded threads per the guide on the serger used for the projects in this book (photo d)

Here are two types of serged stitches that are not used in this book but are good ones to know about:

- Cover stitch (photo e)
- Flat lock stitch (photo f)

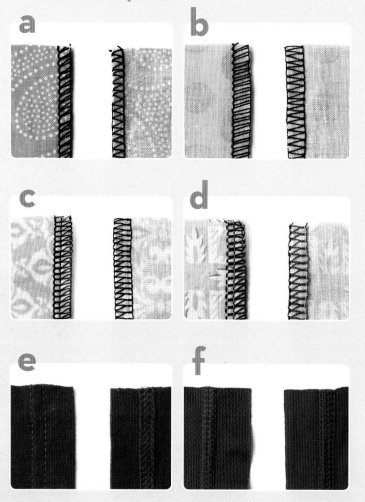

- The **upper blade** goes up and down like the top blade on a pair of scissors (photo 2). The **lower blade** is stationary and works in conjunction with the upper blade to cut the fabric that is being serged (photo 3).
- The **left needle** (farthest away from the blades) anchors the looped threads and makes the 6 mm overlock stitch. It can be used alone or with the right needle.
- The **right needle** (closest to the blades) anchors the looped threads and it makes the 4 mm overlock stitch when used alone.
- The **upper looper** (photo 4) places the thread onto the top of the fabric in small loops or angles. It is the thread color that you see the most when looking at the top of a serged seam.
- The **lower looper** (photo 5) places the thread on the underside of the fabric in small loops or angles.
- The **feed dogs** are the teeth of the machine that grip and pull the fabric along. Usually sergers have a front and back set of feed dogs. They come up through the throat plate.
- The **handwheel/pully** (photo 6) allows you to manually work the machine. Upon the completion of threading or at the start or end of sewing, turn it toward you to pull the needle up to the highest point.
- All threads pass through **tension dials** (photo 7) to put tension on the thread. This helps to create a balanced stitch. Minor adjustments can be made if you are having trouble with a serged seam. Refer to your owner's manual.

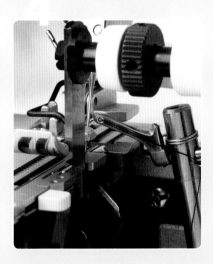

Defining Key Words

- **Serger:** a machine that uses loopers, needles, and three, four, or five threads to make variations to the overlock stitch, cover stitch, and flat lock stitch. There are professional-grade machines designed for just two-thread serging and also some machines that use more than five threads. For the projects in *Serge It!* we will use either three or four threads.

- **Overlock:** the stitch made with a serger. Some people use the words *overlock* and *serger* interchangeably, or say "overlock machine" to mean "serger." In *Serge It!*, the word *serger* will be used to refer to the machine, and the word *overlock* or serge will refer to the general stitches made with the serger. Other types of stitches, such as the cover stitch and flat lock stitch are shown on the left under Serged Stitches.

- **Single needle:** the stitch made with a sewing machine that uses a bobbin and needle. Though technically a serger can be used with a single needle, when we refer to a single-needle machine, it will mean a sewing machine.

Basic Serging Tool Kit

If you have basic sewing skills, you probably have most of the following items needed to make the projects in this book:

- Serger
- Threading tweezers and small screwdriver (to change the thread on a serger; typically these come with the machine)
- Cones of thread for the serger
- Sewing machine and assorted needles

- Thread for the sewing machine
- Scissors
- Straight pins
- Rotary cutter, quilter's ruler, and self-healing cutting mat
- Sharp craft knife
- Fabric spray adhesive
- Measuring tape

- Hand-sewing needles, including a large-eye darning needle
- Iron and ironing board
- Water-soluble fabric marker or sharp pencil
- White pencil
- Fray retardant

- The **presser foot** (photo 8) is directly above the feed dogs and puts pressure on the fabric as it's being serged. It does not move, but you can change out the presser foot with different kinds for different effects.
- The cones of thread rest on the **spool holders** (photo 9).
- Thread gets pulled through the **thread guide** (page 10) before traveling in through the loopers and needles.
- The **presser foot pressure knob** (photo 11) adjusts the pressure on the presser foot.
- The **stitch length dial** (photo 12) adjusts the length of the stitch, which needs to change depending on the thickness of the fabric. For example, when working with denim, the stitch length in general will be longer than when working with chiffon. But stitch length needs to work in conjunction with presser foot pressure. Check your owner's manual to find out the standard stitch length recommended for most serged projects.

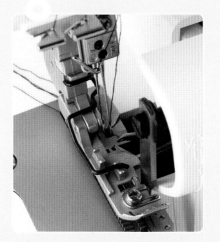

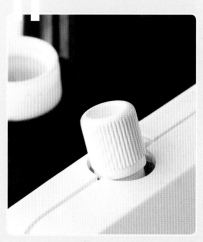

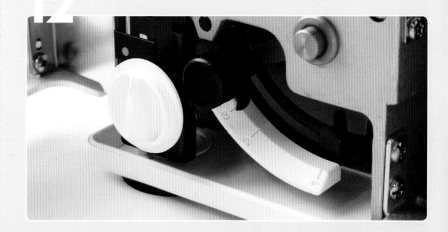

Similarities and Differences Between a Serger and Sewing Machine

When you first look at a serger, you will see that there are parts to it that look like a sewing machine as well as parts that don't look like a sewing machine at all. There are key ways in which the two machines are similar and different:

KEY SIMILARITIES

- The serger and sewing machine use needles, threads, and feed dogs to make stitches on fabric. They both have dials and knobs that allow you to adjust tension and stitch length.
- The serger and sewing machine both have a hand wheel on the right-hand side to help manually move needles, loopers, feed dogs, and threads along.
- The serger and sewing machine both operate with a presser foot.

KEY DIFFERENECES

- The serger does not use bobbins. Rather, it uses loopers that create curvy or angular loops of thread that are placed onto the fabric. These loops of thread are stitched down with either one or both serger needles.
- The serger comes with an upper blade and lower blade that function together to cut the fabric (much like a pair of scissors would) at the same time that the fabric is being stitched. The sewing machine does not come with any blades and therefore does not cut the fabric while sewing. Some modern sewing machines do have blades that cut threads at the end of a seam. *Note:* If you were to run a piece of fabric through a serger without any threads, the blades would end up trimming the edge of the fabric without stitching it.
- Because the serger has a left- and right-hand needle, using one or both affects the stitch width. Sewing machines don't have cutting widths because they do not cut fabric as they

Key Serger Adjustments

Tension: The tension dial on some sergers ranges from 1 to 9, with the standard tension ranging from 3 to 5. The dial range on your serger may differ, so read your owner's manual to find out what the standard tension range is for your machine. The tension should be adjusted according to the weight, and thickness of the fabric you are using. (Generally, a thick fabric requires a loose tension and vice versa.) On the serger used for this book, you turn the dial to a lower number to loosen the tension and to a higher number to tighten the tension. For example, when working with a thick denim, the tension may need to be set at 1 or 2. When working with a sheer organza, the tension may need to be set at 8 or 9.

Stitch Length: The standard stitch length for some sergers is between 2 and 3. Again, the standard stitch length for your machine may differ so you'll want to read your owner's manual. The stitch length is increased for thicker fabrics and shortened for thinner fabrics.

sew. *Note:* Keep in mind that seam allowance (area between the fabric edge and the stitch line) is different than the cutting width (area between the cut fabric edge and the right-most serged line). Usually, a part of the seam allowance will be cut away by the blades as fabric is being serged.

All About Threads

Sergers can use a lot of different kinds of threads. Serger thread is labeled as such and is generally a core-spun polyester. This thread comes on cones and can be used in both the needles and loopers. It is generally finer than all-purpose sewing machine thread, which helps reduce the bulk of a serged seam.

After you take a class from a local shop, most likely you will end up bringing your threaded serger home. That's good news, because when a machine is pre-threaded, and once you know how to use the knot-and-pull method (below), you will most likely never have to rethread it from scratch.

KNOT AND PULL RETHREADING

This method provides steps to follow when you are ready to rethread all cones on the serger. Before trying this method, refer to your owner's manual to find out if there is a particular order you must follow in terms of which cone to start with or end with. For example, the owner's manual for the serger (used for the projects in this book) explains the order as follows: upper looper, lower looper, right-hand needle, and then left-hand needle.

1 Snip the first thread close to the cone (photo 13).

2 Remove the old cone of thread off the spool holder.

3 Place the new cone of thread onto the spool holder (photo 14). Tie the end of the old thread to new thread in a double knot (photo 15).

4 Repeat steps 1 through 3 for all other threads.

5 With the presser foot up and the needles fully raised, loosen the serged thread tail that is coming out from under the presser foot so that all the threads are free. You may want to use the threading tweezers (see Basic Serging Tool Kit, page 12) to untangle the thread tail.

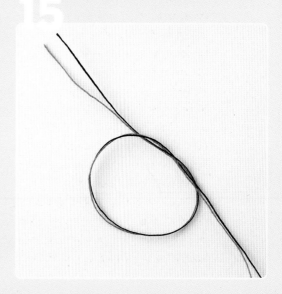

Anatomy of a Serged Seam

You will notice that the upper looper and lower looper threads are the ones you see most visibly on a serged seam. These two threads are the ones that get used up the fastest. If you only have two cones of thread that match the fabric you are stitching on, put those cones on the upper and lower loopers.

If you don't like changing the thread, you can choose to change just the upper looper thread when needed, which is the thread most visible from the right side of the fabric. If you don't care how the thread looks on the back side of the fabric, you might not want to bother changing the lower looper thread. If you see that a looper thread is running low, change that cone to one of the needle threads.

Sergers usually have parts and pieces that are color-coded so that you can see how each thread travels through the serger.

6 Pull the threads that are coming out from the eye of the needles. This is important because the knotted threads will not be able to pass through the eye of the needles.

7 Gently pull the first thread and carefully nudge the knot through the tension dial. You may need to coax the knot through by gently pulling it back and forth with both hands until the knot passes through the dial.

8 For the first needle thread, after passing it through the dial, snip the thread at the knot and then thread the needle. Repeat for the second needle thread.

ONE THREAD CHANGE

If you are changing only one thread, repeat step 5 to loosen the serged thread tail. Give each thread a tug to find out which thread you need to cut, knot, and pull. Your serger will most likely have color-coded parts and pieces with color-coded diagrams on the actual machine to help you identify which thread needs changing. Once you identify which one you need to change, repeat steps 1 through 4 for just the thread that you are changing.

Note: Once everything has been threaded and all threads are under the presser foot, be sure to lower the presser foot, and run the serger to create a length of serged thread tail. This is an important step. Don't start without serging a thread tail in the front of the fabric.

WORKING WITH FEWER THREADS

Sometimes the project you are working on requires fewer threads than are already on your serger. In those situations, we recommend that you find a way to tuck the nonrequired thread and needle out of the way rather than completely unwinding the thread(s) from the machine. Here's an example of how a thread and needle can be tucked out of the way on the serger (photo 16).

THREADING YOUR MACHINE FROM SCRATCH

Whether you need to change one or all threads, the steps for the Knot and Pull method and One Thread Change method are all you will need to do. As long as you carefully tie the ends of the two threads together and gently guide that double knot through all the parts and pieces, you will never have to thread the machine from scratch.

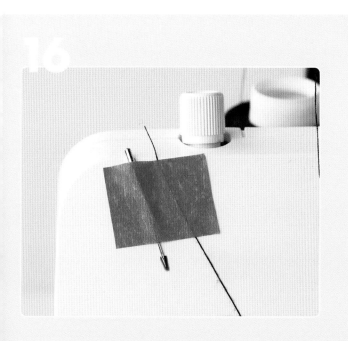

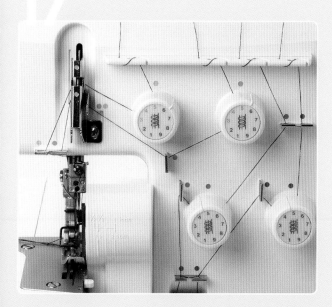

Of course the thing about "never" is that sometimes you run into an unexpected problem. For example, when a thread breaks in the middle of a project, you may have to actually thread the serger from scratch. If this does happen, your three best friends will be your owner's manual, your threading tweezers, and your serger.

Typically, the instructions in the manual will correspond with color-coded parts (photo 17) and other diagrams on the serger to help you thread the machine from scratch. The two most important things to keep in mind are to:

1 Go in the order instructed by your owner's manual.

2 Make sure that the thread is engaged in every tension dial.

If all else fails and you simply cannot thread the serger from scratch, you can always take it into the shop where you learned your basic information and ask them to help you thread your machine. If this does happen, take lots of notes, and perhaps even some photos or video clips along the way.

techniques and terms

If you've never used a serger, you will be learning new methods as you make the projects in this book. This section serves as a guide for terms and techniques you may not be familiar with, as well as a reminder for some you may already know.

Single-Needle Stitching

Basting stitch: This is a long, temporary stitch usually used to hold a seam together. A basting stitch is also used when fabric is being gathered up, as is the case with the top edge of the apron project, page 124. The basting stitch length for most sewing machines is 4.

Stay stitch: This is a single line of stitching, usually near the cut edge of a single layer of fabric where there is a bias cut. The purpose of the stay stitch is to keep the fabric edge from stretching out and becoming distorted. The stay stitch length for most sewing machines is 4.

Serger Stitching

Turning corners: To turn at an outward corner (photo 18), stitch right up to the edge of the fabric and then take one stitch off the fabric. You will want to use the hand wheel to make this one stitch. Lift the presser foot and loosen the needle threads from the tension knobs to create a little bit of slack. Turn the fabric, releasing the thread from the stitch finger and align the fabric under the presser foot. Then lower the presser foot and continue stitching.

Rolled edge: Every serger is going to require different things to happen in order to make a rolled edge. On some sergers, you move the overlocking width selection knob forward, and change the serger to 3-thread mode with the right needle only, and use a standard foot. The thread tension may need to be adjusted and the stitch length is usually shortened, but the specifics on how to make a rolled edge on your machine will be explained in your owner's manual.

Clean-Finishing

At the beginning and the end of a serged seam you will have a serged tail of threads. Clean-finishing the serged thread tails is very important. As a rule of thumb, if a project is going to be washed, use the large-eye needle method; if the project will likely never be washed, then use the fray-retardant method.

Large-eye needle method: Thread a large eye needle with the serged tail and then tunnel it back through the serged seam (photos 19 and 20).

Fray retardant method: Fray retardant is a clear liquid that can be applied to threads and seams to stiffen them. Sometimes the retardant may discolor the fabric, so carefully apply a small dot of the fray retardant only on the thread tail right where it comes off of the fabric. Once the retardant is completely dry, snip the serged tail off, close to the fabric (photos 21 and 22).

18

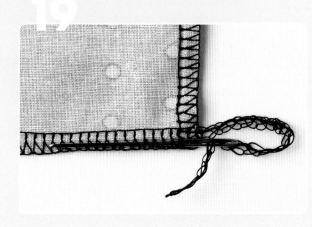

19

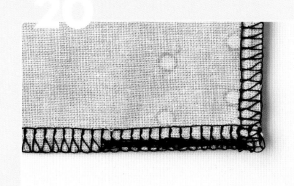

20

21

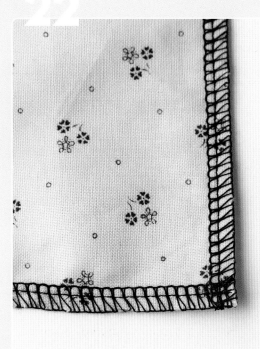

22

Handy Hand Stitches

A handful of embroidery and hand stitches are used in a few of the projects, some of which serve a useful purpose and some of which are decorative. This handy chart shows all the stitches you'll need to know for this book.

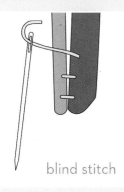

blind stitch

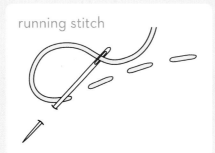

running stitch

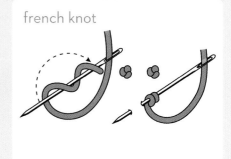

french knot

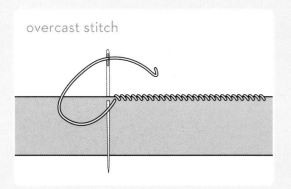

overcast stitch

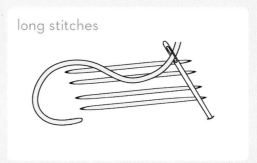

long stitches

Tips and Tricks

Here are some tips and tricks that you'll want to keep in mind as you are making the projects in this book.

SHEER V. HEAVY FABRICS

All sergers come with a factory-adjusted pressure for serging standard-weight quilting cotton. The machine sometimes needs to be adjusted from this standard pressure when working with fabrics that are lighter or heavier. When working with sheer fabrics, the presser foot pressure needs to be decreased. Conversely, for thick or heavy-weight fabrics the presser foot pressure needs to be increased.

A serger also comes with upper and lower loopers adjusted to standard settings. When working with sheer fabrics the loopers may need to be tightened, and likewise loosened when working with thicker fabrics.

True Up Occasionally, instructions will ask you to true up the fabric. This means to make a piece of fabric or a layer of fabrics straight, and true to grain by cutting or ripping the thickness(es) along the grainline.

NEEDLES

For most of the projects in this book, use standard universal sewing machine needles (size 80/12); however, there are exceptions. For instance, when the Wrap-Tie Top (page 96) was being constructed, small holes formed where the needle had punctured/cut the fabric. The standard needle was replaced with a ballpoint needle, which solved the problem. Just like with sewing, let your fabric guide you to change needles to accommodate the weight and type of fabric you are serging.

Most sergers are designed to work with standard/universal sewing machine needles (size 80/12). These standard needles are good for serging quilting cotton as well as woven and knit fabrics in a wide range of weights. However, there are some serger models that require special serger needles. If this is the case for your serger, you may want to use a size 60/8 needle for sheer fabrics and a size 120/19 needle for heavier fabrics.

PRESSER FOOT

Most serger presser foot pressure comes adjusted for standard medium-weight fabrics. That standard pressure can be adjusted—increased for thicker fabrics and decreased for sheer fabrics. On some sergers, there are no marks or numbers that correspond to light or heavy pressure but there is a way to set it back to standard. Every serger is different, so refer to your owner's manual to adjust pressure as needed, and don't forget to bring it back to standard after finishing a project that required an adjustment.

SERGED SEAM AS DECORATIVE ELEMENT

Most of the projects in this book use serged seams as decorative elements, deliberately exposing and setting off the serging with contrasting threads. For example, the thread colors selected for the apron project (page 124) add interest by using black thread on the needle, gray on the upper looper, and pink thread on the lower looper. If you wanted to change the look of the exposed seam, change the thread color on the upper looper only—this is the thread you see the most in projects with exposed seams. Remembering this will help you better understand how the serger works and how you can make an immediate change in a decorative element.

For the internal serged seams, make sure to match the needle thread color to the fabric. In this case, the thread colors for the loopers aren't important because those threads are on the inside and won't be seen, but the needle thread might be seen when the seam is pulled open.

ROTATING THREADS

You may decide to work with a limited number of thread colors, such as black, white, and tan. Limiting thread color options can actually feel rather liberating. Keep in mind that the top and bottom loopers of a serger use up the most thread. So if you are changing from black thread to white and then back to black again, rotate the cones so the thread will be used up at an equal pace.

how to use this book

The first thing you'll want to do is to select a project to make. The projects are not presented in order of difficulty. Rather, they are all prepared for the beginner in mind, but with a design sensibility that will make it super fun for those with a lot of experience.

Templates

Templates for several projects can be found starting on page 134. Here is some information about how to use them.

CUTS AND MARKS

Be aware that some template pieces need to be cut on the fold of the fabric and will be noted as such. Be sure to transfer all markings to the cut pieces of fabric and use them to make notches, or any necessary seam or placement marks.

SIZING

Some templates can be photocopied "as is" and used without any change in sizing. A few templates, however, need to be photocopied at an enlarged size, indicated by a percentage amount. Also, some templates (for example the House Shoes on page 46) have cut lines that allow you to make the project at different sizes. Pay attention to these cut lines when cutting out multiple pieces, to make sure they are all matching in size.

SEAM ALLOWANCE

The templates (as well as measurements for cut pieces without templates) all have seam allowances already added. A minimal amount of fabric will be cut off as you are serging. If a project calls for the machine to have 3 threads and the left needle, then note that the measurement or template already has that stitch width added and that only a sliver of fabric should be cut away as you are serging.

Preparing Your Serger

At the beginning of each project, you'll see a section called "Serger Setup" that looks like this:
- Needles: 1 or 2
- Stitch Width: 6 mm or 4 mm
  - Left needle: Black thread
  - Right needle: Black thread
  - Upper looper: Black thread
  - Lower looper: Black thread

This example tells you to set up your serger with both the left- and right-hand needles in place, and to have black thread loaded onto both needles and both loopers. You don't need to do anything to adjust the stitch width; the notation is simply provided so you know it. If you use both needles, the stitch width will be 6 mm.

Here's another example:

- Needles: 1
- Stitch Width: 4 mm
    - Right needle: White thread
    - Upper looper: White thread
    - Lower looper: Black thread

In this case, you'll know that only the right-hand needle will be used, so the left needle should be removed. Given this, the thread for the left-hand needle will also need to be removed but does not need to be removed from the machine altogether, (see Working with Fewer Threads, page 16). And because only the right-hand needle is being used, the stitch width will be 4 mm. If the threads in your serger have all been black, you'll want to use the knot-and-pull method (page 15) to change the right-hand needle and the upper looper to white thread.

Sometimes projects in this book (such as the Circular Ruffle Scarf Set, page 29) ask you to prepare your serger a certain way, and then to change it at a certain step, for instance, changing one of the thread colors or removing one of the needles. After a project such as this, when you change the machine back, put the needle back in and then thread the tucked thread back into the eye of the needle.

Go for It!

Once your serger is prepared for the project you have selected, you'll want to gather your Basic Serging Tool Kit (page 12) along with any other items found in the Gather list. For the few projects that require templates, make copies at 100 percent or enlarged if indicated. Then, it's time to go for it!

Don't be discouraged if you end up making some mistakes at first. Trial and error is part of the learning process—especially when dealing with a machine with so many moving parts and pieces!

beyond serge it!

The world of serging is much broader than what we have covered this book. There are different feet that you can attach to a serger, specialty threads, and matters related to differential feed. Although our projects do not involve these things, we want to mention them so you know there is a vast world of possibilities to explore.

SPECIALTY THREADS

Decorative metallic thread, wooly nylon thread, and variegated heavy cotton threads can also be used on sergers. These specialty threads should be used on the loopers only, not the needles.

DIFFERENTIAL FEET ATTACHMENTS

As with single-needle sewing machines, a number of presser feet are available to help with different serging needs:

- The **blind stitch presser foot** creates invisible hems while trimming and finishing off the hem edge.
- The **gathering presser foot** is used to join two layers of fabric while gathering or shirring one of the layers.
- The **piping presser foot** allows piping to be laid into a seam while trimming and finishing off the seam.
- The **elastic foot** has a guide to allow elastic to be sewn onto the edge of the fabric while being stretched and without cutting into the elastic.

DIFFERENTIAL FEED

On most sergers, there will be a differential feed knob that adjusts the amount of fabric that is fed to the front feed dogs and to the back feed dogs. Gathering and stretching fabrics can be manipulated by adjusting this knob.

In its normal/standard setting, the differential feed knob on some sergers is set at an N. As the knob is turned toward the right (1.5/2), the feed dogs move at a faster rate than the back feed dogs. This shift prevents stretchy fabrics from getting wavy or stretched out. If puckering occurs while serging a project, it is recommended that the differential feed knot be turned toward the left (.07) which will cause the front feed dogs to move slower than the back feed dogs, thus preventing the puckering.

The location of differential feed knobs differs on all sergers and whether you turn it right or left may also differ. So be sure to read your owner's manual to understand how to adjust your differential feed as needed.

The handwritten note on the label reads: "Happy Birthday Sierra"

stash fabric gift wrap with tag

Got stash fabric? Then this is the perfect project for you. Gather all of your treasured bits and pieces of fabric to make a gift wrap that is also a gift in itself.

Gather

- Basic Serging Tool Kit (page 12)
- Stash fabric in a variety of colors, 26 inches (66cm) long
- Scrap of batting: 4½ x 3 inches (11.4 x 7.6 cm)
- 2 scraps of osnaburg fabric: 4½ x 3 inches (11.4 x 7.6 cm) each
- 1 transparency sheet cut to 4 x 2½ inches (10.2 x 6.3 cm)
- 1 piece of cardstock cut to 3½ x 2¼ inches (8.9 x 5.7 cm)
- Gift box: 10 x 12 x 2 inches (25.4 x 30.5 x 5.1 cm)
- Double-sided fashion tape (available at department stores and online)

* *Osnaburg is a plain fabric historically made from flax yarns. The fabric looks like linen but is usually less expensive. Today, osnaburg is most commonly made from cotton and used for quilting, home décor, and apparel projects. It is widely available at most fabric stores.*

Serger Setup

(see Preparing Your Serger, page 22)

- Needles: 1
- Stitch width: 4 mm
  - Right needle: Black thread
  - Upper looper: Taupe thread
  - Lower looper: Taupe thread

Finished Dimensions:

Gift Wrap: 24 x 26 inches (61 x 66 cm)

Tag: 4½ x 3 inches (11.4 x 7.6 cm)

Make

1 Cut stash fabric pieces to make 11 strips that are all 26 inches (66 cm) long and vary slightly in width, from approximately 1¾ to 4 inches (4.4 to 10.2 cm) (photo 1, page 28). If you have pieces that are not long enough, piece two or more strips together by putting them wrong sides together and serging the short ends.

2 Pin two strips with wrong sides together, and serge. Add the next strip, wrong sides together, and serge again. Continue until all strips have been serged together.

3 Press the serged cloth, making sure all seams go in the same direction, then serge around the outer perimeter (photo 2, page 28).

4 Clean-finish all serged thread tails using the fray retardant method (page 18).

5 Use fabric spray adhesive to sandwich the batting between the two pieces of osnaburg. Serge across one short end. Then serge across the other short end and continue down one long side. When you reach the edge, serge without any fabric or batting to create a 6-inch (15.2 cm) serged thread tail for a loop for the tag, and then serge the other long side (photo 3, page 28).

6 Cut fabric scraps from your stash as follows:
- 2 pieces that measure 2 x ½ inches (5.1 x 1.3 cm) each
- 2 pieces that measure 4 x ½ inches (10.2 x 1.3 cm) each

Place a short fabric scrap on top of the transparency, aligned with one of the short sides, and serge. Place a long fabric scrap on top of the transparency on a long side, overlapping the first strip, and serge. Repeat until all fabric scraps have been serged onto the transparency (photo 4).

7 Clean-finish all serged thread tails using the fray retardant method.

8 Center the serged transparency onto the osnaburg and single-needle stitch them together on all but the short side closest to the loop.

9 Write a sentiment onto the cardstock and insert it into the tag through the short open end.

10 Cut, serge, and true up fabric scraps to make one long strip that measures 1½ x 48 inches (3.8 x 121.9 cm). Clean-finish all serged thread tails using the fray retardant method.

11 Wrap the gift box with the fabric wrap. Use double-sided fashion tape to hold the fabric together in key spots, and then use the long strip from step 10 to tie the gift, making sure to attach the tag.

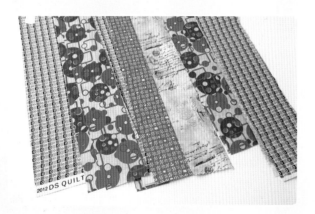

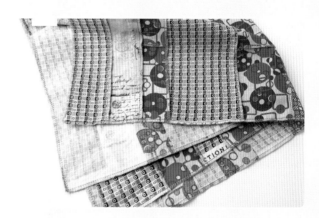

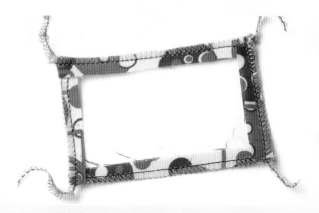

circular ruffle scarf set

For a dramatic statement, stack and wear all three ruffled scarves at once, or wear just one or two scarves at a time for a more understated look.

Gather

- Basic Serging Tool Kit (page 12)
- Templates A, B, and C (page 135)
- ⅔ yard (61 cm) of gray polyester chiffon
- ¼ yard (22.9 cm) of white polyester chiffon

Serger Setup

(see Preparing Your Serger, page 22)
- Needles: 1
- Stitch width: 4 mm
  - Left needle: White thread
  - Right needle: White thread
- Upper looper: White thread
- Lower looper: White thread

Finished Size:

7 x 66 inches (17.8 x 167.6 cm)

Make

1 Use the templates to cut the following pieces:
- Template A: 5 circles from gray chiffon
- Template B: 6 circles from white chiffon
- Template C: 6 circles from gray chiffon

Transfer the cutting line and center hole to the pieces as indicated on the templates.

2 Cut open each circle at the cutting line and then cut out all circle centers so that each piece becomes a split, open ring shape (photo 1).

3 To make the first ruffled strip, stack one of the A pieces on top of another A piece with cut edges aligned. Serge the two pieces together at one

straight-edge cut line (photo 2). Repeat this step until all A pieces are serged together as one long wavy strip that is not joined at the ends.

4 Repeat step 3 with all the B pieces to make a second ruffled strip.

5 Repeat step 3 with all the C pieces to make a third ruffled strip.

6 Change your serger setup as follows:
• Needles: 1
• Stitch width: 4 mm
  ▪ Right needle: White thread
  ▪ Upper looper: White thread
  ▪ Lower looper: White thread

7 Read your owner's manual to change the settings on your serger for a rolled hem. On the serger used for this project, the change involves moving a lever on the thread plate to the up position. On other sergers, you may need to remove the throat plate and add an attachment.

Use this new setup to serge a rolled hem on all interior and exterior curves of the first ruffled strip. Repeat for the second and third ruffled strips.

8 Clean-finish all serged thread tails using the fray retardant method (see page 18).

Tip As you are serging the rolled hem in step 7, you will be cutting off ⅛ of an inch (3 mm) in the process. When you are working on the tiny inner circle areas (concave curves), do not try to pull or tug the fabric. Instead, let the serger grab the fabric and do its thing. It will feel a little bit scary at first, but the more you let the machine do the work without pulling the fabric, the better it will look.

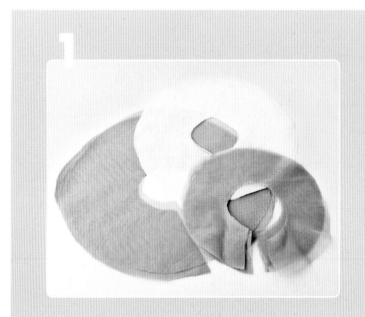

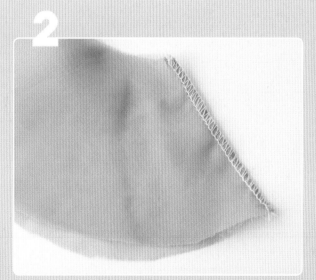

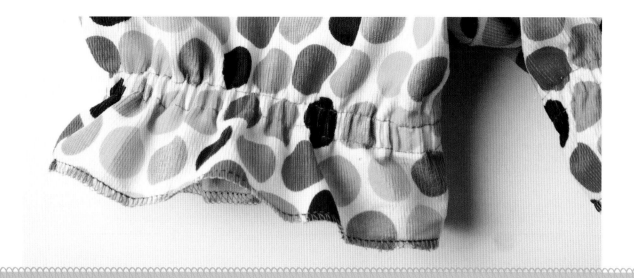

child's bloomers

One of the trickiest parts in making these bloomers is measuring and observing the direction of the corduroy's fuzzy nap. Once you've got that down, you'll be able to serge and stitch soft and cozy bloomers that your child will want to wear every day.

Gather

- Basic Serging Tool Kit (page 12)
- Template (page 142)
- ½ yard (45.7 cm) of fine-wale corduroy
- 1 yard (.9 m) of single-fold bias tape
- Safety pin
- ⅝-inch (1.6 cm) elastic (for the waist)
  - Small: 20 inches (50.8 cm) long
  - Medium: 21 inches (53.3 cm) long
  - Large: 22 inches (55.9 cm) long
- ¼-inch (6 mm) elastic (for the legs)
  - Small: 2 pieces, each 10½ inches (26.7 cm) long
  - Medium: 2 pieces, each 11¼ inches (28.6 cm) long
  - Large: 2 pieces, each 12 inches (30.5 cm) long

Serger Setup

(see Preparing Your Serger, page 22)

- Needles: 1
- Stitch width: 4 mm
  - Right needle: Brown thread
  - Upper looper: Pink thread
  - Lower looper: Pink thread

Finished Sizes:

Child's small, medium, or large, per template cut lines

Make

1 Enlarge the template and cut two pieces out of the corduroy that are mirror images of each other. This can be done in one of two ways:

- Fold the fabric in half and cut through both layers at once.
- Place the template right side up onto the corduroy and cut, and then place the template right side down onto the corduroy and cut a second piece.

Transfer all markings onto the wrong side of both fabric pieces.

Note: Corduroy has distinctive lines in the fabric, made from a process where fibers are twisted (or tufted) and woven. This results in a fabric that looks and feels fuzzy and has a nap. This nap is directional in that it goes in a certain direction. Be mindful of the direction of the nap when cutting and sewing corduroy so that it all goes in the same direction.

2 Prepare the legs:

- Serge the lower leg opening on one piece of corduroy (photo 1).
- Pin the single-fold bias tape to the wrong side of the serged fabric, centering the tape over the placement line. Trim the ends as needed.
- Single-needle-stitch the top and bottom edges of the bias tape to the fabric (photo 2).
- Repeat for the other piece of corduroy.

3 Place the bloomer sides together, right sides facing, and serge the front and back seams (photo 3). Then serge around the entire top edge.

4 To make the top casing, fold under the top edge ¾ inch (1.9 cm) and pin. Leave a small opening at the center back, placing double pins at the start and stop of the opening (photo 4). Single-needle-stitch the folded top edge, making sure to backstitch at the double pins to leave an opening for the elastic.

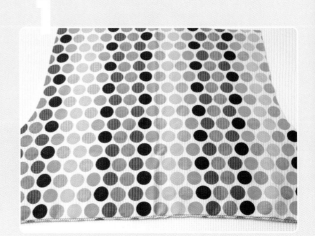

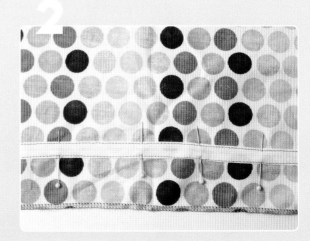

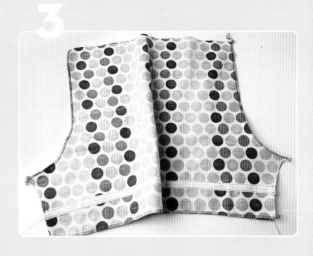

5 Funnel the ⅝-inch-wide (1.6 cm) elastic for the waist through the top waist casing using a safety pin (photo 5). When the elastic comes back out of the casing, slightly overlap the short ends and single-needle-stitch them together. Single-needle-stitch the small opening closed.

6 Funnel one of the thinner ¼-inch-wide (6 mm) elastic pieces through the leg casing created by the bias tape. Pin both ends and then single-needle-stitch across the bias tape, backstitching to secure (photo 6). Repeat for the other leg opening.

7 Serge the crotch area together (photo 7).

8 Clean-finish the serged threads with the large-eye needle method (page 18).

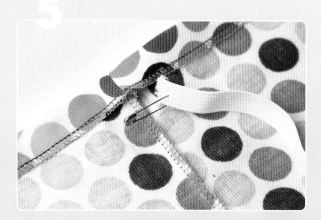

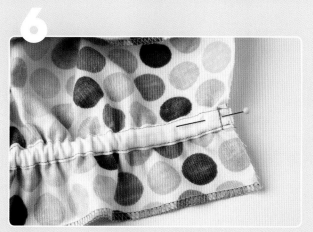

laminated cotton tote

This fashionable tote is made of laminated cotton, which resists stains and moisture while retaining the vibrant colors and patterns of the fabric. Serging and sewing this fabric is easy—just use strips of tissue or a specialty foot to help guide it along.

Gather

- Basic Serging Tool Kit (page 12)
- ¼ yard (22.9 cm) of pink chevron patterned laminated cotton
- ⅛ yard (11.4 cm) of green patterned laminated cotton
- ⅓ yard (30.5 cm) of pink floral patterned laminated cotton
- ¼ yard (22.9 cm) of 12-gauge vinyl
- 4 sheets of tissue paper, 20 x 26 inches (50.8 x 66 cm) each
- 30 silk flowers, sizes from 1 to 3 inches (2.5 to 7.6 cm) in diameter
- Chopstick
- Teflon foot (optional)

Finished Dimensions:

10½ x 14 x 3½ inches
(26.7 x 35.6 x 8.9 cm)

Serger Setup

(see Preparing Your Serger, page 22)

- Needles: 2
- Stitch width: 6 mm
    - Left needle: White thread
    - Right needle: White thread
    - Upper looper: Pink thread
    - Lower looper: Pink thread

How to Sew Laminated Cotton

Placing tissue paper on top of the laminated cotton helps slide the fabric through the serger. Without it, the laminated cotton sticks to the presser foot and does not pass through. If you find it difficult to push the fabric through the serger even with the tissue paper, you may have to add a strip of tissue paper underneath the fabric to prevent it from sticking to the throat plate as well. An alternative to using tissue paper is to get a Teflon foot for your serger.

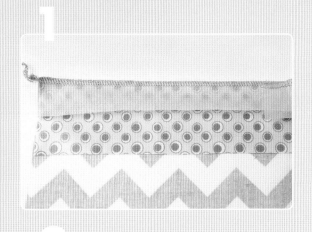

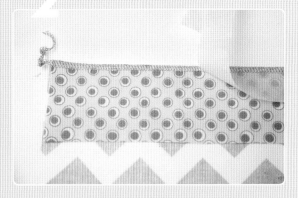

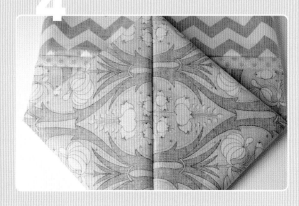

Make

1 Cut the laminated cotton, vinyl, and tissue paper into the following pieces:

- Top strip: 2 pieces of pink chevron laminated cotton, 15 x 6 inches (38.1 x 15.2 cm)
- Middle strip: 2 pieces of green laminated cotton, 15 x 1¼ inches (38.1 x 3.2 cm)
- Bottom strip: 2 pieces of pink floral laminated cotton, 15 x 11 inches (38.1 x 27.9 cm)
- Straps: 2 pieces of vinyl, 2 x 36 inches (5.1 x 91.4 cm)
- Approximately 50 strips of tissue paper, 1½ x 26 inches (3.8 x 66 cm)

2 Sew the front of the bag:

- With wrong sides together, put one of the green strips on top of one of the pink chevron pieces, aligning the long sides together. Put a tissue paper strip on top of the green strip and serge through all thicknesses (photo 1).
- After serging is finished, tear off the tissue paper and discard (photo 2).
- With wrong sides together, put one of the pink floral pieces on top of the nonserged long side of the green strip, aligning the long sides together. Put one of the tissue paper strips on top of the pink floral fabric and serge through all thicknesses. Tear off the tissue paper and discard, then flatten out the pieces (photo 3).
- Repeat to make the back of the bag.

3 With wrong sides together and the pink chevron fabric pieces aligned at the top, serge the front and back units together down one side, across the bottom, then up the other side.

4 Make the boxed corners:

- Turn the bag inside out and fold it so that the bottom seam lines up with one of the side seams and the bottom of the bag looks like a diagonally rotated square (photo 4).

- Measure 1½ inches (3.8 cm) up from the bottom point of the square and make a clean, straight, precise line with a quilting ruler and pencil (photo 5).
- Single-needle-stitch along the pencil line, backstitching at the start and end points. Make sure the bottom seam allowance goes one way and the side seam allowance goes the opposite way to reduce bulk.
- Repeat for the opposite point of the square bottom.

5 Turn the bag right side out. Allow the bag to naturally form a box shape on the sides and bottom. On the front of the bag, fold the fabric 1¾ inches (4.4 cm) from the point where the serger needle made the side seam. Single-needle-stitch as close to the fold as possible, approximately ¹⁄₁₆ inch (1.6 mm) away. Repeat for the other side edge and bottom edge (photo 6). *Note:* If your single-needle machine has a walking foot attachment, then there is no need to use the tissue paper for the single-needle stitching.

6 Finish the top edge:
- Place the tissue paper on the right side of the top edge of the bag and serge across (photo 7). Tear and discard the tissue paper.
- Turn the top edge down by 1¼ inches (3.2 cm) then single-needle-stitch across the top (photo 8).

7 Make the strap:
- Tear apart the silk flowers and cut them into single petals (photo 9).
- Fold one of the vinyl strips in half lengthwise (long sides together). Place a strip of tissue paper on top of the vinyl and serge through all thicknesses on the non-folded long side for approximately 3 inches (7.6 cm).
- Stop and insert a few silk flower petals into the vinyl. Serge another 3 inches (7.6 cm) to cover the inserted petals and then stop to insert a

few more silk flower petals into the vinyl (photo 10). Continue doing this until you reach the end of the vinyl.
- Return to the first 3 inches (7.6 cm) of the serged vinyl and stuff petals into that end with a chopstick.
- Repeat this process with the other vinyl strip to make a second strap.

8 Attach the straps:
- Place the short nonserged end of the first vinyl strap into the groove between the seam made with the pink chevron and green pieces, 2 inches (5.1 cm) in from the folded and stitched side edge. Single-needle-stitch the strap in place (photo 11).
- Do the same for the opposite end of the strap, 2 inches (5.1 cm) in from the folded and stitched edge on the other side.
- Push the serged seam up and single-needle-stitch the two portions of the seam that lie right above where the straps have been stitched down, making sure to backstitch at the start and stop.
- Repeat for the second strap.
- Single-needle-stitch the straps at the top hem line and the fold line, backstitching at all start and end points (photo 12).

kid's fish rug

Kids will love this colorful and cuddly fish made of terry cloth and flannel—all serged and stitched with cute little flapping scales.

Gather

- **Basic Serging Tool Kit (page 12)**
- **Templates A through H (page 140)**
- **½ yard (45.7 cm) of blue terry cloth**
- **⅓ yard (30.5 cm) of coral flannel**
- **1 piece of lime green terry cloth, 25 x 8 inches (63.5 x 20.3 cm)**
- **1 piece of cream terry cloth, 20 x 8 inches (50.8 x 20.3 cm)**
- **1 piece of yellow terry cloth, 8 inches (20.3 cm) square**
- **1 scrap piece of cream felt, 3 inches (7.6 cm) square**
- **½ yard (45.7 cm) of brown terry cloth**

Serger Setup

(see Preparing Your Serger, page 22)
- **Needles: 1**
- **Stitch width: 6 mm**
  - **Left needle: Orange thread**
  - **Upper looper: Brown thread**
  - **Lower looper: Brown thread**

Finished Dimensions:

40 x 18 inches (101.6 x 45.7 cm)

Make

1 Use the templates to cut out the following pieces:
- Template A (body): 1 piece from blue terry cloth
- Template B (face): 1 piece from coral flannel
- Template C (inner collar): 1 piece from lime green terry cloth
- Template D (outer collar): 1 piece from cream terry cloth
- Template E (tail): 1 piece from coral flannel
- Template F (inner tail): 1 piece from green terry cloth
- Template G (scales): 4 pieces from yellow terry cloth and 2 pieces from cream terry cloth
- Template H (eye): 1 piece from cream felt

2 Cut long thin strips as follows:
- 1 from coral flannel, ¾ x 22 inches (1.9 x 55.9 cm)
- 1 from blue terry cloth, ¾ x 10 inches (1.9 x 25.4 cm)
- 1 from lime green terry cloth, 1 x 10 inches (2.5 x 25.4 cm)

3 Serge the outer curve of one of the yellow scales (piece G) and then serge the straight side of the scale (photo 1 on next page). Repeat this step for the other five scales. *Note:* Clean-finish all other serged thread tails for this project using the large-eye needle method (page 18).

4 Serge both long sides of the long coral strip. Equally divide and cut this strip into five pieces. Serge across one short side on two pieces.

5 Make the inner tail:
- Serge around all sides of the green terry cloth inner tail (piece F).
- Position two coral strips aligned with the long curved edge on the tail and trim the strips as needed.
- Single-needle-stitch all four sides of both strips onto the tail fin (photo 2).
- Serge the coral tail fin all the way around.

6 Center the inner tail onto the straight edge of the coral tail fin (piece E). Single-needle-stitch in place (photo 3).

7 Make the inner collar:
- Serge around the outer curve and two short ends of the lime green inner collar (piece C).
- Position the three remaining coral strips onto the inner collar and trim the strips as needed. Serge one short end of all three strips and reposition them on the collar with serged ends aligned with the serged curve. Single-needle-stitch the strips in place (photo 4).

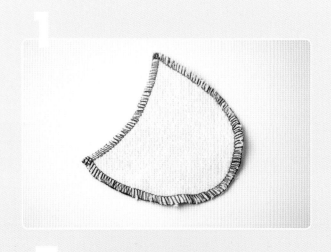

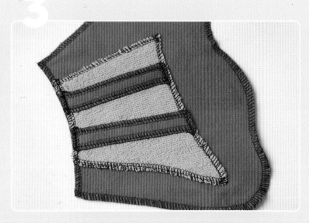

8 Make the outer collar:
- Serge around the outer curve and two short edges of the cream outer collar (piece D).
- Serge both long sides of the long blue strip. Equally divide and cut the strips into four pieces.
- Position the four strips onto the outer collar and trim the strips as needed. Serge one short end of all three strips and reposition them on the collar with the serged ends aligned with the serged curve. Single-needle-stitch the strips in place.

9 Serge around the entire coral face piece.

10 Assemble the face and collar on the cut blue terry cloth. Place the cream collar down, then the green collar slightly overlapping the cream. Place the coral face so that it slightly overlaps the green collar. Adjust the pieces to fit just inside the blue terry cloth with a bit of blue showing on all sides. Pin these layers, then single-needle-stitch the pieces in place. (The eye will be added later.)

11 Assemble the tail:
- Position the tail piece from step 6 onto the tail section of the blue terry cloth and single-needle-stitch in place.
- Serge both long sides of the green terry cloth strip. Position it on the blue terry cloth tail as shown, slightly overlapping the coral and green tail piece.
- Trim the short ends as needed, then serge them.
- Reposition the strip on the tail and single-needle-stitch it in place.

12 Attach the scales:
- Position the serged scales onto the body portion of the blue terry cloth, using the photo as a placement guide. Notice the curved stitch lines on the finished fish that run along the top edge of the scales, and place the scales accordingly. In the rows of two and three scales, allow the top corners to touch each other.

- Starting with the top row, single-needle topstitch across the scales in a curved line, catching all three petals on their straight serged sides. Do not stitch the curved portions of the scales down.
- Repeat with the remaining rows of scales.

13 Place the blue fish onto the brown terry cloth and pin (photo 5). Cut the brown terry cloth ½ inch (1.3 cm) away from the blue serged edge. Remove the blue terry cloth fish and serge around the entire edge of the cut brown terry cloth.

14 Position the blue terry cloth fish back onto the brown outline and single-needle-stitch in place.

15 Single-needle topstitch the eyeball onto the coral face. Also add topstitching along the arched curve of the coral face, around the tail fin, and across the body at the scales, to secure the fish to the brown backing.

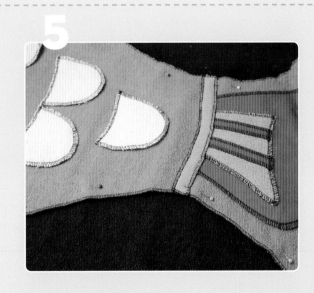

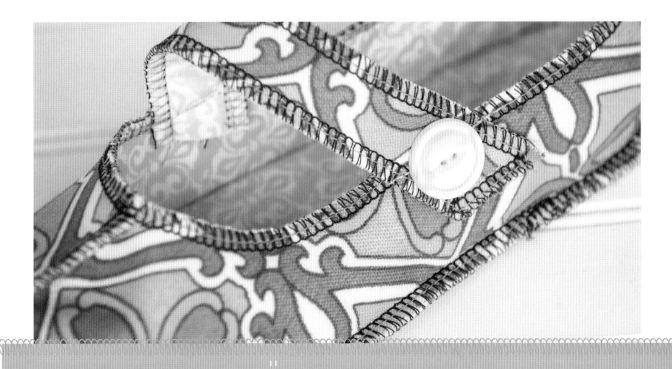

house shoes

Home-decorating fabric makes these shoes durable on the outside, while a coordinating cotton fabric makes them soft, cool, and cozy on the inside.

Gather

- Basic Serging Tool Kit (page 12)
- Templates A, B, and C (page 135)
- ⅓ yard (30.5 cm) of orange/blue patterned home-decorating fabric
- ⅓ yard (30.5 cm) of coordinating aqua patterned quilting cotton fabric
- ⅓ yard (30.5 cm) of fusible fleece
- 2 buttons, 1-inch (2.5 cm) diameter

Serger Setup

(see Preparing Your Serger, page 22)

- Needles: 2
- Stitch width: 6 mm
  - Left needle: Brown thread
  - Right needle: Khaki thread
  - Upper looper: Brown thread
  - Lower looper: Gold thread

Finished Size:

Woman's small, medium, or large.

- -

Make

1 Enlarge the template for size small. If you are making size medium or large, cut the template pieces along the lines indicated and spread the pieces by the amounts listed for your size. For all sizes, check your foot against the template to make sure the pieces match your foot with enough extra room for a ¼-inch (6 mm) seam allowance on all sides. Make any necessary adjustments to the template before cutting out the fabric.

2 From each template, cut the following number of pieces from the home-decorating fabric (see Fabric Note), the quilting cotton, and fusible fleece. Transfer toe and heel notches and strap placement markings to the cut pieces as noted on the templates:

- Template A (sides): cut 4 of each
- Template B (sole): cut 2 of each (mirror pieces) for left and right
- Template C (straps): cut 2 of each; one set needs to mirror the other for left and right straps

Fabric Note If you are using a home-decorating fabric with a pattern, you can fussy-cut to make sure that the pattern is symmetrically mirrored on the outer sides. "Fussy-cut" means cutting patterned fabric to deliberately center or feature aspects of the design. For the shoes shown, the flower-like design is centered on both sides of the toe seam.

3 Following manufacturer's instructions, iron fusible fleece onto the wrong side of each piece of home-decorating fabric for the soles, sides, and straps.

4 With wrong sides facing, place each fused piece onto a matching lining piece, pin, and single-needle baste-stitch with a ¼-inch (6 mm) seam allowance (photo 1). Do this for all pieces.

5 Assemble the sides:
- With linings facing, place the sides of each shoe together and pin. For both shoes, single-needle-stitch a seam at the toe (center front) and heel (center back) with a ¼-inch (6 mm) seam allowance. Remove pins as you go.
- Serge the stitched toe and heel seams (photo 2).

6 Assemble each shoe:
- With linings facing, place a serged top piece onto a sole, matching the toe and heel seams with the notch marks. Pin first at the toe and heel, then add more pins along the heel area, at approximately ½-inch (1.3 cm) increments.
- Place a pin into one of the stitches on either side of the serged center front seam to draw up and gather stitches at the toe. This will help to ease or absorb the extra fabric. Use lots of pins in the toe area to join the two pieces (photos 3 and 4).
- For the right shoe, push both serged seams to the right and single-needle baste-stitch with a ¼-inch (6 mm) seam allowance. For the left shoe, push the serged seams to the left and repeat.

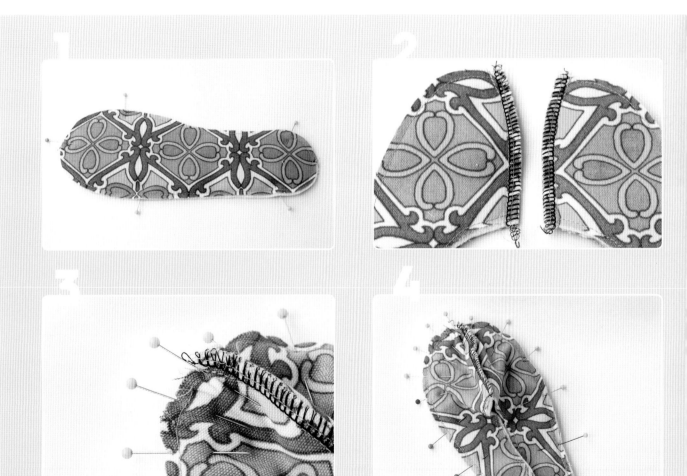

7 Serge both shoes:

- Serge along the top edge, pushing the serged seams in the same direction as before. Notice that the lower looper thread color (gold in the sample) is now showing on the lining inside the shoe.
- Serge along the bottom edge, pushing the serged heel seam in the same direction as before (photo 5).

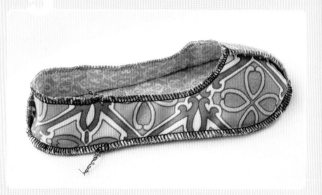

8 To finish each strap, serge along one long side, the short angled side, and the second long side (photo 6).

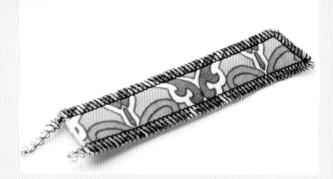

9 Attach the straps to each shoe:

- With exterior side facing up, match up each strap with the correct shoe; as you're looking down at the shoes, the short raw edge will be sewn to the inside edge, with the stitched angled end on the outside edge.
- Refer back to the template as needed to locate the placement notch for the inside (raw) edge of each strap, and pin the straps in place.
- Place your foot into the shoes to make adjustments for the strap placement as necessary and pin the finished end of each strap at a placement that best fits your foot. The button is decorative, not functional, so you want to be able to easily slip your foot in and out of the shoe.
- Single-needle-stitch each strap at both ends with a straight stitch (photo 7).

10 Hand-sew a button to the strap on the outside edge of each shoe (photo 8).

composition book cover

Serging and overstitching gives this book an elegant texture. Once you get the hang of it, you'll want to make several to use and give as gifts.

Gather

- Basic Serging Tool Kit (page 12)
- ⅓ yard (30.5 cm) of linen
- ⅓ yard (30.5 cm) of fusible fleece
- Composition book: 7½ x 10 inches (19 x 25.4 cm)

Serger Setup

(see Preparing Your Serger, page 22)

- Needles: 2
- Stitch width: 6 mm
  - Left needle: Black thread
  - Right needle: Black thread
  - Upper looper: Periwinkle thread
  - Lower looper: White thread

Finished Dimensions:

7½ x 10 inches (19 x 25.4 cm)

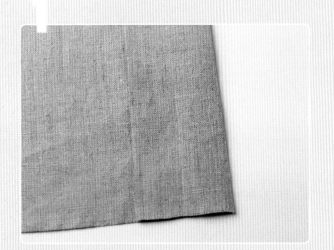

Make

1 Cut the linen and fleece as follows:
- 1 outer piece from linen: 17¾ x 10½ inches (45.1 x 26.7 cm)
- 2 inner flap pieces from linen: 5 x 10½ inches (12.7 x 26.7 cm) each
- 1 piece from fusible fleece: 15¾ x 10½ inches (40 x 26.7 cm)

2 Make the serged "pleats":
- Place the outer linen piece horizontally on your work surface, wrong side up. Fold over the right-hand side by 2 inches (5.1 cm) so that wrong sides are together and press (photo 1).
- Turn the pressed piece over and serge on the fold (photo 2). This allows for the periwinkle thread to be visible.
- Fold the fabric again 1¼ inches (3.2 cm) from the first serged seam and press. Serge on the fold as before (photo 3).
- Repeat this step two more times.

Press all serged seams to the right.

3 Follow manufacturer's instructions and iron the fusible fleece to the back side of the linen outer piece. Trim any excess fleece.

4 Add the wavelike single-needle stitching:
- Use a water-soluble marker to make a column of four dots to the right of the first serged seam (very close to the seam) from the top edge as follows: 1½ inches (3.8 cm), 4 inches (10.2 cm), 6½ inches (16.5 cm), and 9 inches (22.9 cm).
- Make a column of three dots to the left of the fourth serged seam (very close to the seam) from the top edge as follows: 2¾ inches (7 cm), 5¼ inches (13.3 cm), and 7¾ inches (19.7 cm).
- Use the columns of dots as guides to single-needle-stitch back and forth over the seams as shown (photo 4).

5 Serge one long side of one of the inner flap pieces. Repeat for the second inner flap (photo 5).

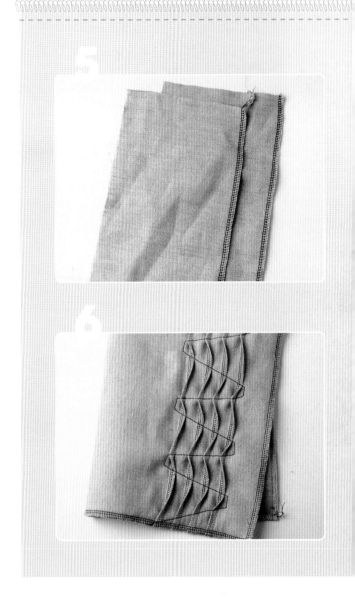

6 Place the outer linen piece on your work surface, wrong side up. Pin the inner flaps onto the short sides, wrong side facing down, with the nonserged long sides of the flaps aligned with the outer piece. Turn this over and serge along the entire perimeter of the outer cover, removing pins as you go (photo 6).

7 Clean-finish all serged thread tails using the fray retardant method (page 18).

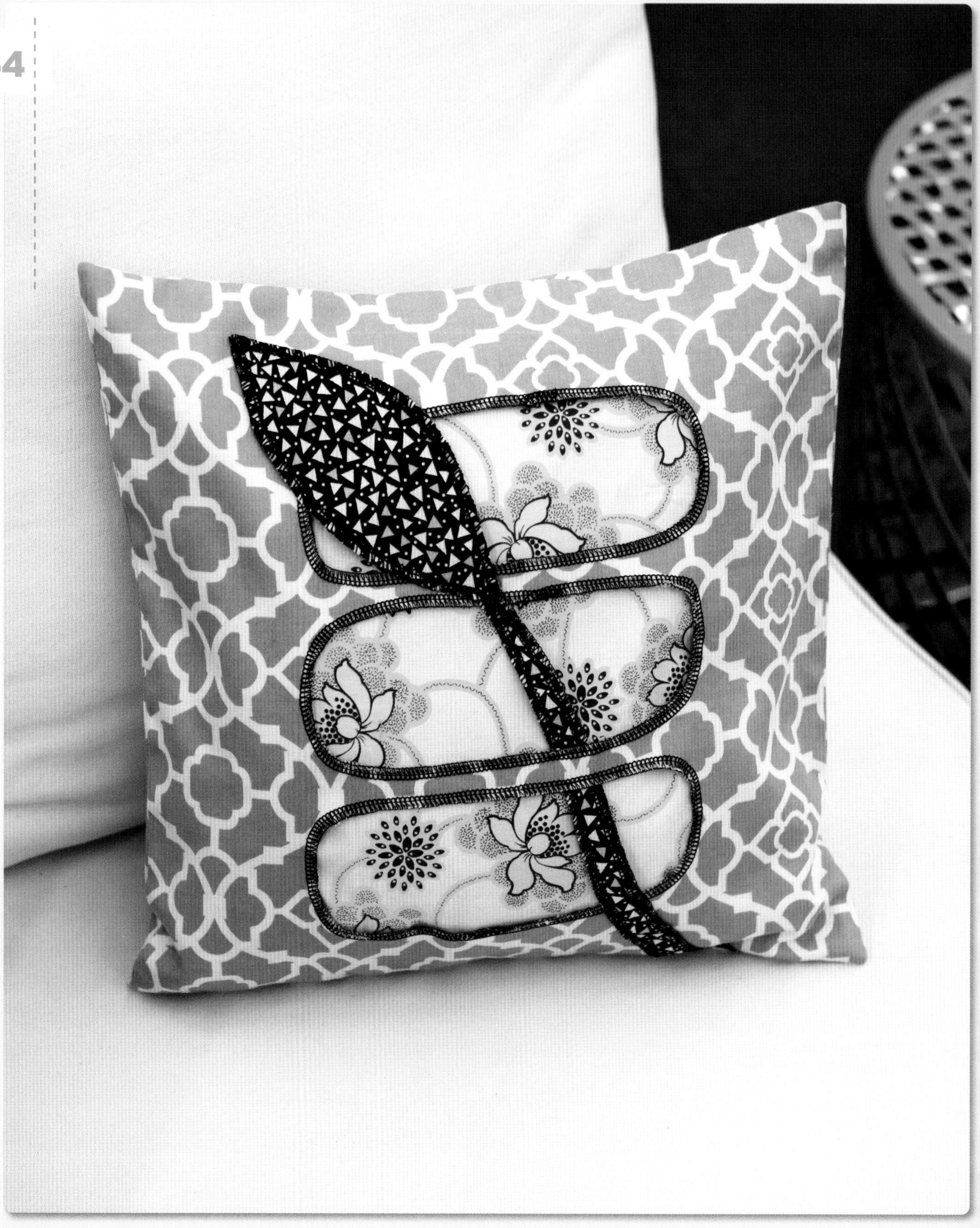

peek-a-boo pillow

Make the inner pillow with two different fabrics, so you can change what peeks through the outer case depending on the season or occasion.

Gather

- Basic Serging Tool Kit (page 12)
- Templates A, B, and C (page 139)
- ½ yard (45.7 cm) each of two patterned quilting cottons (green and coral) for the inner pillow
- Pillow form, 14 inches (35.6 cm) square
- ½ yard (45.7 cm) of turquoise patterned home decorating cotton
- Piece of black patterned fabric (for leaf and stem), 12 x 6 inches (30.5 x 15.2 cm)
- Lightweight fusible interfacing, 12 x 6 inches (30.5 x 15.2 cm)

Serger Setup

(see Preparing Your Serger, page 22)

- Needles: 2
- Stitch width: 6 mm
  - Right needle: Black thread
  - Left needle: Black thread
  - Upper looper: Black thread
  - Lower looper: Black thread

Finished Dimensions:

15 inches (38.1 cm) square

Make

The Inner Pillowcase

1 Cut both inner pillow fabrics into 16-inch (40.6 cm) squares.

2 With right sides facing, pin the squares together, starting slightly left of center at one side and ending about 4 inches (10.2 cm) before the start. Double-pin at the start and end points (photo 1).

3 Single-needle-stitch around all sides, using a ½-inch (1.3 cm) seam allowance and backstitching at the start and end points.

4 Trim the corners at a diagonal (photo 2) and turn the pillowcase right side out (photo 3). Press.

5 Push the pillow form into the pillowcase through the opening (photo 4).

6 Tuck in the seam allowance at the opening and pin. Topstitch the opening closed (photo 5).

The Outer Case Front

1 Cut the exterior fabric into the following pieces:
- 1 front piece, 16 inches (40.6 cm) square
- 2 back pieces, each 10½ x 16 inches (26.7 x 40.6 cm)

2 Enlarge the templates. On the wrong side of the front square:
- Pin template C horizontally 3½ inches (8.9 cm) up from bottom edge and centered side to side (photo 6). Trace with a pencil.
- Now pin the template 3½ inches (8.9 cm) down from the top edge, once again centered, and trace.
- Center the template between the first two tracings and once again trace.

3 Cut out the three traced shapes.

4 Shorten up the serger's stitch length. Every serger is different, but for this project the stitch length was shortened to 2. Just like on a sewing machine, the smaller the number for the stitch length, the closer together the stitches are. Slowly serge around all three ovals (photo 7). Straighten the fabric out at the curves and pull it outward while serging it. If the fabric remains curved, the serger's blade will cut the fabric.

5 Clean-finish all serged thread tails using the fray-retardant method (page 18).

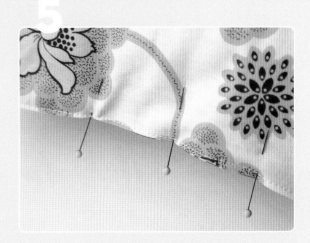

The Leaf and Stem

1 Use templates A and B to cut the leaf and stem shapes from the black patterned fabric and from the lightweight fusible interfacing.

2 Following the manufacturer's instructions, press the interfacing to the back side of the fabric pieces.

3 Serge along the entire outer edge of the leaf. For the stem, serge the two long sides and leave the two short sides unserged (photo 8).

4 Clean-finish all serged tails on the leaf using the large-eye needle method method (page 18).

5 Weave the stem in and out through the ovals of the pillow cover and pin. Pin the serged leaf on the cover, slightly overlapping the top of the stem (photo 9). Single-needle-stitch the stem and leaf down, only on sections where it meets the outer case front.

Finish the Outer Pillow

1 Press and stitch a ¼-inch (6 mm) double-fold hem on one long edge of both back pillow pieces (photo 10).

2 Lay the pillow front on a flat surface, right side facing up. With right sides together and the hemmed edge on the left, pin one of the backs to the right edge as shown (photo 11). Pin the other back on the opposite side, right sides facing and the hemmed edge on the right. The two back pieces will overlap by 4 inches (10.2 cm). Pin the pieces together on all sides (photo 12).

3 Stitch around the perimeter of the outer cover with a ½-inch (1.3 cm) seam allowance, pivoting at the corners.

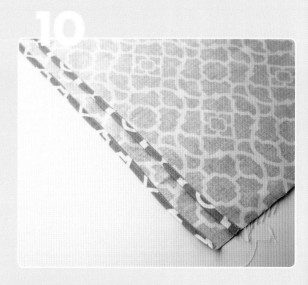

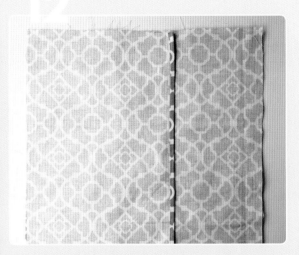

4 Trim the corners at a diagonal and turn the outer pillow right side out. Press.

5 Insert the inner pillow into the outer pillow cover (photo 13).

Tip Change the mood of the room by flipping the inner pillow to allow either the green or coral fabric to peek through.

upcycled sweater skirt

To make this eye-catching wrap-style skirt, find a bargain sweater from the thrift store that you can cut up into parts and pieces.

Gather

- Basic Serging Tool Kit (page 12)
- 1 wool or wool-blend sweater*
- Tailor's chalk
- Approximately 36 inches (91.4 cm) of black lace hem tape, ¾ inch (1.9 cm) wide**
- Approximately 36 inches (91.4 cm) of black elastic, ½ inch (1.3 cm) wide**
- Safety pin
- Pink perle cotton
- 3 black buttons, approximately 1-inch (2.5 cm) diameter (they don't need to match in size)

*   *To make sure the sweater is large enough, measure the circumference of the bottom hem of the sweater, which will become the waistline of the skirt. You'll need enough for your waist measurement plus at least 10 inches (25.4 cm) for the overlap in front. You will use elastic to reduce the overlap to 8 inches (20.3 cm); because the sweater is stretchy, the waistline also needs to be stretchy. Wool or wool-blends tend to hold their shape better than cottons or linens. Heavier-weight sweaters will add bulk, so a medium- to lightweight sweater is best. Consider a sweater that has a pattern knit into it, such as Fair Isle. Flip the sweater upside down and see how you like the pattern running in a different direction. Because of the construction of sweater, the pattern will end up upside down.*

** *The best gauge for the actual length of the lace and elastic is the measurement of your waist plus 8 inches (20.3 cm) for the overlap. If you want the skirt to ride lower, say closer to your hip, take the waistline measurement at that location.*

Serger Setup

(see Preparing Your Serger,
page 22)

- Needles: 2
- Stitch width: 6 mm
  - Left needle: Light pink thread
  - Right needle: Bright pink thread
  - Upper looper: Light pink thread
  - Lower looper: Light gray thread

Finished Size:

*A man's size medium sweater was used to
make a woman's size small sweater skirt.*

Make

1 Lay the sweater out flat on your work surface.
Cut the sweater into parts as follows (photo 1):

- Cut freehand straight across the body of the
  sweater, front and back, just beneath the
  armholes (photo 2). The lower body of the
  sweater (A) will become the body
  of the skirt.
- Cut off the sleeves just inside the armhole
  seams.
- Cut off the neckband at the seam line. The
  upper sweater is B.

Note: After the sweater has been cut up, handle the pieces carefully to avoid stretching them too much. When the pieces are serged together, the serging will prevent any unraveling from happening.

2 Lay A flat, with the side seams in place on the sides and the former "top" of the sweater at the bottom. Measure and mark the center front, at both the top and bottom edges, with a pin. Use tailor's chalk and a ruler to draw a line between the marks and cut straight up the center front. Draw rounded bottom corners with chalk and cut with scissors (photo 3).

3 Try on the skirt by wrapping it around your body at your preferred waistline and overlapping one side (right over left, as you are wearing it) by at least 10 inches (25.4 cm). If it feels too big, keep in mind that the elastic can gather up to 9 inches (22.9 cm) of extra length. However, more than that will make for a bulky waistline. If you need to trim down the front edges a bit, or take in the skirt at the sweater side seams, now is the time to do it.

4 From B, cut multiple 1½-inch-wide (3.8 cm) strips. With right sides together, stitch the strips end-to-end to create one long strip that is 75 inches (190.5 cm) long, using a single-needle zigzag stitch.

5 Serge one long side of the continuous strip. To make it ruffly, pull the strip as you feed it through the serger, so the sweater ribs open up. Stop pulling the strip for the last 5 inches (12.7 cm); this end will be on the inside flap of the skirt, and you want it to be less bulky.

6 With right sides together, pin the non-serged long edge of the strip to the outer edge of the skirt, right sides together, starting at the upper right-hand corner of the skirt. The strip will not reach all the way to the top of the upper-left: the right-hand portion of the skirt will wrap over the left-hand portion, and you want the inner skirt to lie flat against the body (photo 4).

7 Serge the ruffle to the skirt.

8 To make a lace casing, pin the lace hem tape to the inside of the waist, easing the stretchiness of the waist to match the lace as follows:
- Start by pinning one end of the lace to one corner of the skirt's waist (photo 5).
- Pin the other end of the lace to the opposite waist corner.

- Find the center point of the lace and the center back of the skirt, and pin those points together.
- Find the halfway points of the lace between the center back and each end, and pin those points at the side seams of the skirt.
- Evenly distribute the top sweater edge between these points and pin at intervals to the lace. Pin, pin, and then pin again, for the best distribution of the sweater to the lace.

9 Single-needle-stitch the lace at both the top and bottom edges to create the casing. Remove the pins as you are sewing.

10 Use an iron to steam any fullness of the sweater into the lace.

Note: Before pinning, this sweater measured 45 inches (114.3 cm) at the waist. After pinning, it measured 36 inches (91.4 cm)—an 8 percent decrease. The lace helps ease in the bulky fullness of the sweater and then the ironing helps to steam flat any fullness of the sweater. The elastic draws the waist back in and helps maintain the desired waist measurement.

11 Clean-finish all serged thread tails using the large-eye needle method (page 18).

12 Use a safety pin to tunnel the elastic through the casing. Pin at the beginning and at the end and tack both ends in place (photo 6).

13 Overlap the skirt, placing the right-hand side over the left-hand side by approximately 8 inches (20.3 cm). Lower the front edge 1½ inches (3.8 cm) from the top edge of the waist. Do the same thing on the inner edge. Pin in place. Single-needle-stitch at the bottom edge of the waist, making sure not to catch the elastic (photo 7).

14 Use a hand-sewing needle and pink perle cotton to attach the three decorative buttons to the skirt.

Idea Use any excess material (for instance, from the sleeves) to make a coordinating serged cuff or hair accessory.

finger-less gloves

Polar fleece is just the right fabric to make these fashionable gloves, because it is soft, warm, and easy to work with. Make several pairs—use fun patterned fleece like the pair shown here or solid-color fleece for a simpler look.

Gather

- **Basic Serging Tool Kit (page 12)**
- **Templates A, B, and C (page 139)**
- **⅓ yard (30.5 cm) of polar fleece**
- **2 medium buttons**

Serger Setup

(see Preparing Your Serger, page 22)

- **Needles: 1**
- **Stitch width: 6 mm**
  - **Left needle: Brown thread**
  - **Upper looper: Brown thread**
  - **Lower looper: Brown thread**

Finished Size:

One size fits most women, per template cut lines

Make

1 Use the templates to cut the following pieces, transferring all markings to the cut pieces as noted on the templates.

- Template A (inner and outer hand): cut 4 (2 mirrored pairs)
- Template B (button flap): cut 2
- Template C (thumb gusset): cut 2

2 Serge three sides of both button flap (B) pieces, leaving one short end unstitched.

3 With both right sides facing up, pin the nonserged edge of a button flap to the inside edge of one of the hand (A) pieces, centered between the placement notches. Baste in place (photo 1). This A piece becomes one of the outer hands. Select a mirrored hand piece for the

opposite outer hand and attach the remaining button flap in the same way.

4 Stretch out the thumb area of an inner hand so that the U becomes relatively straight. With wrong sides together, pin one long side of a thumb gusset (C) to this straightened-out edge and serge. Pin the corresponding outer hand to the opposite long side of the thumb gusset, wrong sides together, and serge. You now have an outer and inner hand connected along the thumb gusset (photo 2). Repeat for the opposite hand.

5 Flatten out the thumb end of the gusset, push the serged seams toward the center, and serge all three pieces as shown (photo 3). Repeat for the opposite hand.

6 Flatten the top edge of the gloves, push the serged seams toward the center, and serge from one side across the gusset to the other side (photo 4). Repeat for the opposite hand.

7 With wrong sides together, serge the outer-edge seam, then serge the inner-edge seam, making sure to catch the button flap.

8 For each cuff, cut 2 rectangles that measure 5 x 11 inches (12.7 x 27.9 cm). Fold with right sides together and the short ends aligned. Serge across the short ends.

9 Attach the cuffs (see the Tip):
- For each cuff, fold in half with wrong sides together, aligning the long edges.
- Pin the cuff inside the arm opening of one of the gloves, aligning raw edges.
- Single-needle baste-stitch the cuffs to the gloves.
- Serge the basted seam through all thicknesses (photo 5).
- Roll up the cuff over the glove (photo 6).

Tip When the cuff is shoved inside the glove in step 9, it will feel awkward because the circumference of the cuff is slightly larger than the circumference of the glove. This may require you to stretch the thicknesses a bit and thoroughly pin before you baste. Once the seam is serged and the cuff is pulled up over the glove, the extra width of the cuff will allow it to sit nicely around the glove. Without the extra width, the cuff would end up choking the glove.

10 Hand-sew a button onto the finished end of each button flap, making sure that you sew through only the button flap and the outer layer of the glove.

11 Clean-finish all serged thread tails using the large-eye needle method (see page 18).

fruity trivets

Felts and flannels form these quirky and colorful trivets that are sure to brighten up your kitchen.

Gather

- Basic Serging Tool Kit (page 12)
- Spray Adhesive
- For the Grapefruit Trivet:
  - Templates A, B, C, and D (page 136)
  - 3 pieces of craft felt, 9 x 12 inches (22.9 x 30.5 cm), 2 dark yellow and 1 white
  - Scraps of flannel in pink, tangerine, and fuchsia
  - White perle cotton
  - Pink perle cotton
- For the Kiwi Trivet:
  - Templates A, B, C, and D (page 136)
  - 2 pieces of craft felt, 9 x 12 inches (22.9 x 30.5 cm), brown and green
  - 1 piece of lime green flannel, 9 x 12 inches (22.9 x 30.5 cm)
  - Scrap of white flannel
  - Polyester fiberfill, a pinch
  - Off-white perle cotton
  - Black perle cotton

- For the Watermelon Trivet:
  - Templates A, B, C, and D (page 137)
  - 3 pieces of craft felt, 9 x 12 inches (22.9 x 30.5 cm), 2 green and 1 fuchsia/red
  - 1 piece of light green flannel, 9 x 12 inches (22.9 x 30.5 cm)
  - Scrap of black felt
  - Black perle cotton

Serger Setup
Grapefruit Trivet

(see Preparing Your Serger, page 22)

- Needles: 1
- Stitch width: 4 mm
  - Right needle: White thread
  - Upper looper: Orange thread then white thread (in step 3)
  - Lower looper: White thread

Kiwi Trivet

- Needles: 1
- Stitch width: 4mm
  - Right needle: White thread
  - Upper looper: Brown then green (step 3) then white (in step 4)
  - Lower looper: White thread

Watermelon Trivet

- Needles: 1
- Stitch width: 4 mm
  - Right needle: White thread
  - Upper looper: Green thread then white (in step 5)
  - Lower looper: White thread

Finished Dimensions:

Grapefruit: 7$\frac{1}{2}$ inches (19 cm)
Kiwi: 8 x 6 inches (20.3 x 15.2 cm)
Watermelon: 9$\frac{1}{2}$ x 5$\frac{1}{2}$ inches (24.1 x 14 cm)

Make

GRAPEFRUIT TRIVET

1 Use the templates to cut the following pieces:
- Template A: 2 circles from dark yellow felt
- Template B: 1 circle from white felt
- Template C: 3 segments each from pink, tangerine, and fuchsia flannel
- Template D: 9 seeds from white felt

2 Spray the back of one of the dark yellow felt circles with spray adhesive and place it on top of the second felt circle. Serge around the outer edge (photo 1).

3 Change the upper looper thread from orange to white and serge around the entire white felt circle.

4 Spray the back side of the white felt circle with spray adhesive and center it on top of the dark yellow felt circle. Single-needle-stitch around the white felt circle to attach it to the yellow felt circle.

5 Find the center point of the piece by folding it in half one way, and then folding it in half the opposite way. Mark the center with the water-soluble pen (photo 2).

6 With the center point as the guide, arrange the nine flannel segments onto the white circle, alternating the colors. Spray the backs of the segments with spray adhesive, one at a time, and adhere them on the circle.

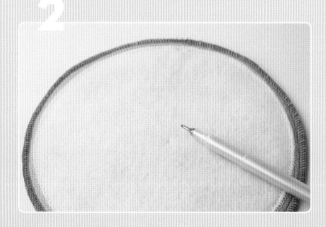

7 Spray the backs of the 9 white felt seeds with spray adhesive and adhere them to the flannel segments, one at a time, and place them on the circle.

8 Overcast-stitch each flannel segment along its outer edge with pink perle cotton and a hand-sewing needle. Make French knots in the middle of the white seeds with white perle cotton and a hand-sewing needle (photo 3).

9 Clean-finish all serged thread tails with the large-eye needle method (page 18).

KIWI TRIVET

1 Use the templates to cut the following pieces:
- Template A: 2 ovals from brown felt
- Template B: 1 oval from green felt
- Template C: 1 oval from lime green flannel
- Template D: 1 center shape from white felt

2 Use spray adhesive to adhere the two brown ovals together. Serge around the outer edge.

3 Change the upper looper thread to green. Serge around the outer edge of the green oval felt.

4 Change the upper looper thread to white. Serge around the outer edge of the lime green oval flannel.

5 Use spray adhesive to stack and attach the brown, green, and lime green serged pieces together. Single-needle-stitch around the edge of both green ovals to sew them all together.

6 Position the white felt shape at the center of the piece. Start overcast stitching around the edge with off-white perle cotton and a hand-sewing needle. When there is a small bit of the shape still

left to stitch, stuff it with a tiny bit of polyester fiberfill and then finish overcast stitching the shape.

7 Stitch around the entire shape with off-white perle cotton with long, exaggerated, and uneven radiated stitches. Make French knots in between the radiated stitches with black perle cotton (photo 4).

8 Clean-finish all serged thread tails with the large-eye needle method (page 18).

WATERMELON TRIVET

1 Use the templates to cut the following pieces:
- Template A: 2 semicircles from green felt
- Template B: 1 semicircle from light green flannel
- Template C: 1 semicircle from fuchsia/red felt
- Template D: 9 seeds from black felt

2 Use spray adhesive to adhere the two green semicircles and serge around the outer edge.

3 Serge around the light green semicircle.

4 Use spray adhesive to center the light green serged semicircle on top of the green serged semicircle, matching the straight edges. Single-needle-stitch around the entire piece to stitch the layers together, including the straight edge.

5 Change the upper looper thread to white. Serge around the outer edge of the fuchsia felt. Use spray adhesive to center it on the green serged and stitched pieces, with straight edges aligned. Single-needle-stitch around the entire serged piece.

6 Use spray adhesive to attach all the black seed pieces to the watermelon piece. Use black perle cotton and a hand-sewing needle to make two French knots on each seed.

7 Clean-finish all serged thread tails with the large-eye needle method (page 18).

ruffled purse

This roomy and eye-catching purse is both practical and bohemian chic—a wonderful accessory that can make everyday outfits feel special.

Gather

- Basic Serging Tool Kit (page 12)
- Template A (page 141)
- ½ yard (45.7 cm) of osnaburg fabric
- ½ yard of floral quilter's cotton
- ½ yard (45.7 cm) of gray polka dot quilting cotton
- ⅓ yard (30.5 cm) of gray polyester suiting
- ⅛ yard (11.4 cm) of printed quilting cotton (for trim)
- ½ yard (45.7 cm) of lightweight fusible interfacing

Serger Setup

(see Preparing Your Serger, page 22)

- Needles: 1
- Stitch width: 4 mm
  - Right needle: Gray thread
  - Upper looper: Taupe thread
  - Lower looper: Gray thread

Finished Dimensions:

18 x 14 inches (45.7 x 35.6 cm)

Make

1 Use Template A to cut out the following pieces needed for the body of the purse:

* 2 pieces from osnaburg
* 2 pieces from floral quilting cotton (lining)

Transfer the ruffle placement marks onto the osnaburg only, using a pencil (photo 1).

2 Cut the following pieces from fabric and interfacing:

* For the front/back tops, cut six pieces that are 2¼ x 13 inches (5.7 x 33 cm): 2 from the floral, 2 from osnaburg, and 2 from interfacing.
* For the side/bottom strip, cut three pieces that are 2 x 41 inches (5.1 x 104.1 cm): 1 from the floral, 1 from osnaburg, and 1 from interfacing.
* For the strap, cut three pieces that are 2 x 43 inches (5.1 x 109.2 cm): 1 from the floral, 1 from osnaburg, and 1 from interfacing.

Tip Depending on the width of your fabric, you may need to piece together strips of fabric to get the desired length. If so, add ¼-inch (6-mm) seam allowances to the strips as needed and single-needle-stitch the short ends of the strips together with right sides facing. You might want to label your pieces in the seam allowance to keep them straight.

3 Following the manufacturer's instructions, fuse the cut interfacing to the wrong sides of the following pieces:

* 2 front/back top pieces of floral quilting cotton
* 1 side/bottom strip of osnaburg
* 1 floral quilting cotton strap

4 Assemble the purse body:

- Place the two fused floral front/back top pieces on top of the corresponding osnaburg pieces, wrong sides together, and serge across one long edge of each set (photo 2). Set aside.
- Pin a floral body to an osnaburg body with wrong sides together and single-needle baste-stitch with a ¼-inch (6 mm) seam allowance around the entire perimeter. Repeat for the remaining body pieces (photo 3).
- Lay the purse body on a flat surface with the osnaburg side facing up. Align one of the top pieces along the top edge, also with the osnaburg side facing up. Serge the top edges together (photo 4).
- Press the top piece upward, with the floral side facing out and the serging on the inside (photo 5).
- Repeat steps to make the purse back.

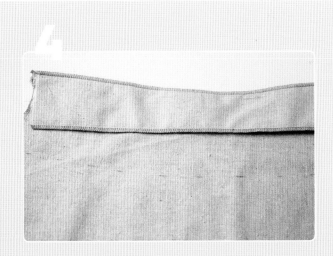

5 Assemble the side/bottom strip and the straps:
- Pin together the short ends of an interfaced floral strap to both short ends of an interfaced osnaburg side/bottom piece. Serge the ends together. You now have a large interfaced ring, with floral fabric on the upper portion of the ring and the osnaburg on the lower portion of the ring. This will be the exterior side.
- Pin the remaining floral strap and side/bottom piece together in the same way. Serge the ends together. This will be the interior side and strap.
- Place the interior ring inside the exterior ring, aligning the strap portions of the same length. Pin and baste the layers together around both edges with a ¼-inch (6 mm) seam allowance.

6 Attach the sides/strap to the purse body:
- With lining sides facing (both are flowered), pin the side/bottom strip to the purse front at the side, around the bottom, and to the other side. Single-needle-stitch together, backstitching at both ends to reinforce where the strap meets the purse body.
- Pin the opposite long edge of the side/bottom to the purse back, and again stitch from one side to the other, backstitching at both ends (photo 6).
- Serge around the entire perimeter of the strap and side/bottom strip on both long edges (photo 7).

7 For the ruffles, cut the following:
- Top ruffle: 1 piece of gray polka dot quilting cotton, 60 x 4¾ inches (152.4 x 12 cm)
- Middle ruffle: 1 piece of gray suiting, 66 x 4¾ inches (167.6 x 12 cm)
- Bottom ruffle: 1 piece of gray polka dot quilting cotton, 72 x 4¾ inches (182.9 x 12 cm)

8 Make the ruffles:
- Fold the fabric strip for the top ruffle in half with right sides together, aligning the short edges.
- Serge the ends together.
- Serge the top and bottom edges of the ring (photo 8).
- Repeat for the middle ruffle and bottom.

9 Gather and attach the ruffles:
- Fold the top ring in half, with the seam on one side; mark the folded edge that is opposite the seam.
- Make two rows of single-needle basting stitches along the top edge of the serged ring, starting at the seam: one at ½ inch (1.3 cm) from the top edge and the other at ¼ inch (6 mm) from the top edge (photo 9).
- With both purse and ruffle facing right side up, pin the double-stitched edge of the ruffle to the front of the purse along the top marked line. Center the surged ruffle seam on a purse side seam, with the opposite marked edge centered on the opposite side of the purse.

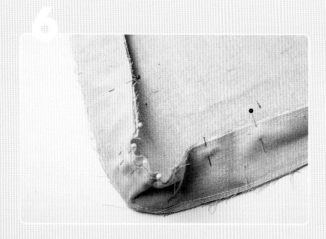

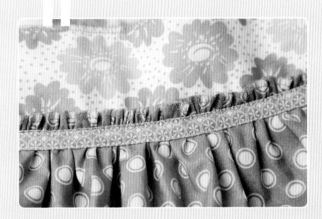

- Gather the ruffle by pulling the top threads of both rows until the ruffle fabric is flush with the purse. Distribute the gathers evenly and pin (photo 10).
- Single-needle-stitch the ruffle all the way around, in between the two rows of basting stitches. *Note:* Feeding the entire piece under the presser foot of the sewing machine requires patience. It can be awkward to get all the layers to go through. Be careful to not stitch through the strap.
- Repeat the process for the middle and bottom ruffles.

10 Prepare and attach the trim:
- Cut a strip from the patterned quilting cotton, 31 x 1 inch (78.7 x 2.5 cm).
- Press under one long edge of the trim ¼ inch (6 mm). Repeat for the other long edge.
- Pin the trim onto the top ruffle to cover the two rows of gathering stitches. Allow the final short end to overlap the starting point and fold it under by ¼ inch (6 mm).
- Single-needle-stitch both the top and bottom edge of the trim, backstitching at both ends (photo 11).

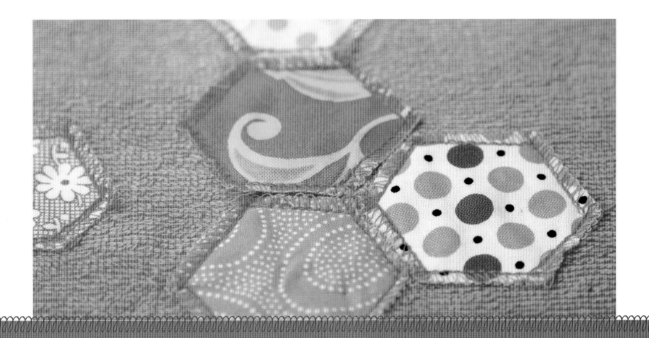

ombré-hexagon burp cloth

Create this burp cloth by first dipping white terry cloth into a dye bath, and then sewing serged hexagons onto the front. It makes a fabulous baby shower gift!

Gather

- Basic Serging Tool Kit (page 12)
- Washer and dryer
- ⅝ yard (.6 m) of 100 percent cotton terry cloth fabric (see Fabric Note on next page)
- Sheet of plastic to protect your floor or work surface
- Liquid dyes: fuchsia and tangerine
- Sink or bucket that can hold 3 gallons of hot water
- Rubber gloves
- Templates A and B (page 134)
- Assorted cotton scrap fabrics
- Fabric glue stick

Serger Setup
Burp Cloth

(see Preparing Your Serger, page 22)

- Needles: 2
- Stitch width: 6 mm
  - Left needle: Orange thread
  - Right needle: Orange thread
  - Upper looper: Orange thread
  - Lower looper: Red thread

Serger Setup, cont.
Hexagons

- **Needles: 1 right needle (for the edges of the hexagons)**
- **Stitch width: 4 mm**
  - **Right needle: Orange thread**
  - **Upper looper: Pink thread**
  - **Lower looper: Pink thread**

Finished Dimensions:

20 x 24 inches (50.8 x 61 cm)

Fabric Note You will be cutting two cloths of equal size from terry cloth. If the fabric width is 55 inches (139.7 cm) or 66 inches (167.6 cm), you can cut two cloths that are 20 x 24 inches (50.8 x 61 cm), the size of the cloths shown, with a bit of fabric left over. If the fabric width is 45 inches (114.3 cm), you can cut two cloths that are 20 inches (50.8 cm) square. Before cutting the cloth, wash and dry without detergent or dryer sheet to relax it.

Make

1 Carefully cut two cloths of equal size on the straight of grain, as much as possible. Washed terry cloth has a tendency to look uneven.

2 Serge the outer edges of the terry cloth, taking care to properly turn corners as you serge (see Turning Corners, page 18). Clean-finish the serged threads using the large-eye needle method (page 18) (photo 1).

3 Cover your floor or work surface with plastic and prepare a dye bath in the sink (or bucket) using 3 gallons (11.4 l) of hot water and half a bottle of fuchsia liquid dye.

4 Soak the terry cloth in room-temperature water and then wring it out. While wearing rubber gloves, scrunch up the terry cloth in the middle and dip only the lower half in the dye bath three times to create a gradated effect as follows:
- Entire half: fast few seconds
- Lower two-thirds: 1 minute
- Lower one-third: 5 minutes

5 Rinse out the terry cloth in cold water until the water runs clear.

6 Repeat step 3 with the tangerine dye and then repeat step 4 also with the tangerine dye bath to create the cloth shown in photo 2.

7 Wash the terry cloth in the washing machine using cold water, and then dry it in the dryer, following manufacturer's instructions for the dye (photo 2).

8 Use template A and assorted cotton fabric scraps to cut out 19 hexagons. Use template B and assorted cotton fabric scraps to cut out two smaller hexagons.

9 Serge around all six sides of each hexagon, allowing the thread tails at either end of each side to hang freely (photo 3).

10 Arrange the serged hexagons on the terry cloth as you would a puzzle, until you like what you see (photo 4).

11 Use a fabric glue stick to secure all tails to the back side of each hexagon (photo 5) and pin all hexagons in place.

12 Single-needle-stitch all hexagons to the terry cloth.

Variations

- Make a burp cloth with fewer hexagons.
- Use just one dye color and leave the opposite side of the burp cloth white.

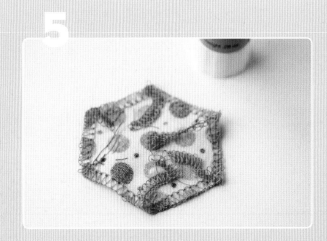

vinyl lunch bag

To make this chic bag, start by carefully cutting the vinyl into the necessary pieces, and then sew the pockets to the front and back sides with a single-needle machine. After that, it's just a few simple serged seams to finish a bag that you can use to carry almost anything.

Gather

- Basic Serging Tool Kit (page 12)
- Masking tape
- ⅓ yard (30.5 cm) of vinyl
- Size 16 regular or leather sewing machine needle
- 2-inch (5 cm) binder clip
- Ephemera for pockets (optional)

Serger Setup

(see Preparing Your Serger, page 22)

- Needles: 2
- Stitch width: 6 mm
  - Left needle: White thread
  - Right needle: White thread
  - Upper looper: White thread
  - Lower looper: White thread

Finished Dimensions:

7 x 12 x 5 inches (17.8 x 30.5 x 12.7 cm)

Make

1 Before you cut the vinyl, tape down one edge onto a self-healing cutting mat with masking tape to stabilize it. Then use a quilter's ruler and rotary cutter to cut the following pieces:

- Front and back (cut 2): 7½ x 12¼ inches (19 x 31.1 cm)
- Sides (cut 2): 5 x 12¼ inches (12.7 x 31.1 cm)
- Bottom (cut 1): 5 x 7½ inches (12.7 x 19 cm)

Also cut 4 pockets to the following sizes:

- 2 x 4 inches (5.1 x 10.2 cm)
- 1½ x 1¾ inches (3.8 x 4.4 cm)
- 1½ x 2½ inches (3.8 x 6.4 cm)
- 4 inches (10.2 cm) square

2 Arrange the three smaller pockets on the front of the bag as desired so that they are approximately 5½ to 6 inches (14 to 15.2 cm) from the top edge. *Note:* There is no need to pin the pockets in place because vinyl is tacky when it touches vinyl.

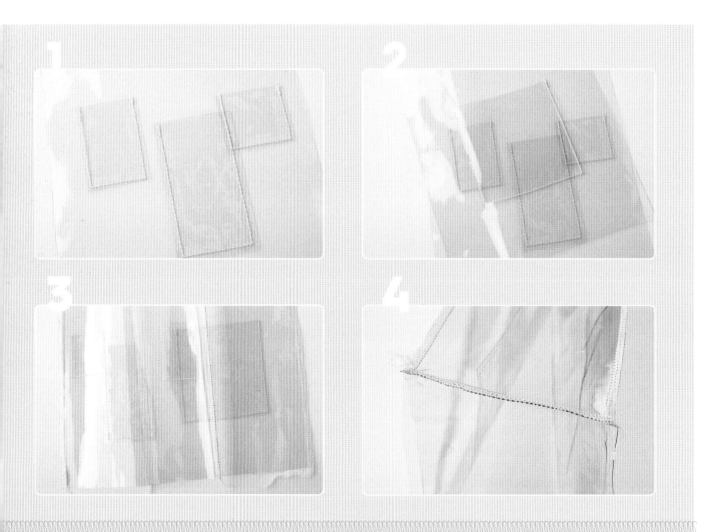

3 Single-needle-stitch the sides and bottom of the first pocket, backstitching at the start and finish, and pivoting at the corners (see Serger Stitching, page 18). Repeat with the other two pockets (photo 1).

4 Center the large pocket on the back of the bag, 6 inches (15.2 cm) from the top. Stitch in place as you did the smaller pockets (photo 2).

5 With right sides facing up, place the front of the bag onto your work area, then a side panel, then the back of the bag, and finally, the second side panel, matching up the long edges. With wrong sides facing, start by serging the bag's front and first side panel together, then continue stitching the long sides together until the bag shape is complete (photo 3).

6 Match up the short ends of the bottom piece to the sides of the bag. With wrong sides together, serge the short ends to the sides (photo 4).

7 Match up the long sides of the bottom with the bag's front and back, and serge as before. At this point, the bag will naturally form a brown-bag fold and the corners will feel thick where all the layers come together (photo 5).

8 Serge the top edges. The top of the bag will naturally fold in on itself into a brown-bag shape.

9 Clean-finish all serged thread tails using the large-eye needle method (page 18).

10 Fold over the top of the bag and secure with a binder clip (photo 6). Slip images into pockets for decoration.

Variation Arrange corresponding pieces of hook-and-loop tape on the back and front of the bag so that they meet when the top of the bag is folded over twice. Single-needle-stitch in place.

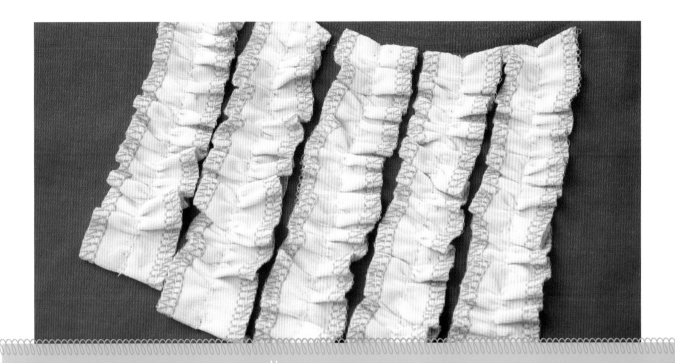

tuxedo tee

Make heads turn by transforming an ordinary tee into a sweet and sassy tuxedo tee. Simply add serged strips that are gathered and sewn in place.

Gather

- Basic Serging Tool Kit (page 12)
- Woman's scoop-neck tee in your size
- 5 strips of jersey knit (cut from an old tee): 1⅛ x 10½ inches (2.8 x 26.7 cm) each

- White cardstock

* *The instructions for this project are for the red tee made with five strips of jersey knit. To make the blue tee, cut 3 strips of patterned cotton fabric: 1½ x 10½ inches (3.8 x 26.7 cm) each.*

Serger Setup

(see Preparing Your Serger, page 22)

- Needles: 2
- Stitch width: 6 mm
  - Left needle: Cream thread
  - Right needle: Cream thread
  - Upper looper: Pink thread
  - Lower looper: Cream thread

Finished Size:

A woman's size small tee was used for this project.

Make

1 Serge both long edges of each fabric strip.

2 Single-needle baste-stitch down the centers of each fabric strip. Be sure to backstitch at the start of each strip, but do not backstitch at the end of the strips; just let the threads run off at the end (photo 1).

3 Fold the tee in half lengthwise—shoulder touching shoulder—to find the center front. Lightly press. Place a pin at the top of the center front at the neckline seam.

4 Measure down 6 inches (15.2 cm) from the first pin and mark with another pin.

5 Fold under the backstitched short end of one serged strip ¼ inch (6 mm) and pin it at the center front with the first pin from step 3.

Tip When pinning the strips onto the tee, place a piece of white cardstock into the tee so that you don't accidentally pin through the back side.

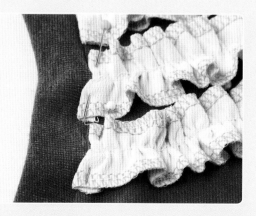

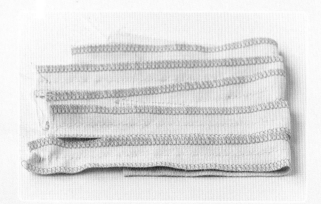

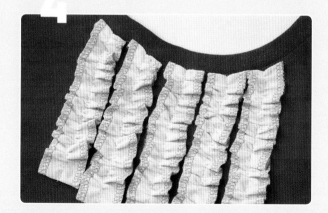

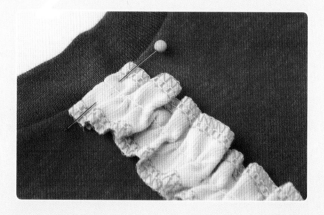

6 Pull the top thread from the other end of the strip and push up the fabric so that it starts to gather. Move the gathers up so that they are evenly spaced (photo 2). Do this until the strip meets the bottom pin. Fold under the bottom edge of the serged strip and then pin in place.

7 Repeat steps 5 and 6 with the other four strips, turning each under at an angle to follow the curve of the neckline and turning the bottoms under at the same angle. Space the strips ¼ inch (6 mm) apart (photo 3).

Tip Use a ballpoint needle when stitching on knit fabrics to prevent little holes from forming.

8 Single-needle-stitch down the center of all strips along the gathering sitch, removing pins as you go. Be sure to backstitch at the start and end of all strips (photo 4).

wonky log cabin clock

The fabric strips in this classic log cabin pattern are irregular in size, adding a bit of wonkiness to the design. This fun twist produces an effect that is more freeform and improvisational than traditional.

Gather

- Basic Serging Tool Kit (page 12)
- Scraps of coordinating fabrics in assorted patterns and weights, such as ticking, home-decorating fabric, lace, cotton, burlap, wool suiting, and felt
- Dark gray perle cotton
- 1 piece of ticking, 10 x 11 inches (25.4 x 27.9 cm)

- 1 piece of batting, 10 x 11 inches (25.4 x 27.9 cm)
- Clock workings*
- 4 pieces of ½-inch-thick (1.3 cm) foam core, 3 inches (7.6 cm) square
- White craft glue
- Museum wax or earthquake putty (available at hardware stores)

*Older clocks found at thrift stores or flea markets sometimes have more interesting workings than brand-new clocks. For this project, a new clock was unclamped and all parts discarded except for the hands and the battery unit, which were attached to the serged clock face.

Serger Setup

(see Preparing Your Serger, page 22)

- Needles: 1
- Stitch width: 4 mm
  - Left needle: Black thread
  - Right needle: Tan thread
  - Upper looper: Tan thread
  - Lower looper: Tan thread

Finished Dimensions:

10 x 11 inches (25.4 x 27.9 cm)

Make

1 Choose the fabric scrap for the center of the clock's face and cut a small rectangle measuring 2½ x 4¼ inches (6.4 x 10.8 cm).

2 With wrong sides together, place this rectangle against a fabric strip that is slightly longer and approximately the same width. Serge together along one long edge. Trim the excess fabric from the strip (photo 1).

3 Open the sewn pieces with right sides facing you. Rotate the block so that the strip you just added is at the top. Push the serged seam toward the front (center) rectangle.

4 With wrong sides together, place the next fabric strip down the right side of the joined rectangles, aligning the edges. Serge the edges together, and push the serged seam toward the center rectangles (photo 2). Trim the excess fabric (photo 3).

5 Repeat steps 2 through 4—serging, trimming, rotating, and adding logs around the edges—until the block is slightly larger than 10 x 11 inches (25.4 x 27.9 cm). Vary the width of the strips to make the block uniquely wonky.

6 True up the pieces to measure 10 x 11 inches (25.4 x 27.9 cm).

7 Freehand cut the numbers 3, 6, 9, and 12 from scrap felt. The numbers should be approximately 1½ inches (3.8 cm) tall. *Note:* In our clock, because the fabric strips on the sides and bottom edge were lighter in color, the numbers 3, 6, and 9 were cut with a darker piece of felt to create

contrast (photo 4). Conversely, because the strip on the top edge was fairly dark, the number 12 was cut with a lighter piece of felt (photo 5).

8 Use a running stitch to secure the numbers onto the serged piece with dark gray perle cotton and a hand-sewing needle (photo 6).

9 Place the ticking on your protected work surface with wrong side facing you and spray a coat of fabric adhesive onto it. Place the batting on top of the ticking and spray a coat of fabric adhesive onto it. Place the serged piece on top of the batting right side facing up. Pin the pieces together at the center (photo 7).

10 Pin and single-needle baste-stitch on all sides through all thicknesses (photo 8).

11 Change Serger Setup as follows:
Needles: 2
Stitch width: 6 mm
- Left needle: Black thread
- Right needle: Black thread
- Upper looper: Black thread
- Lower looper: Black thread

12 Serge around all sides (photo 9).

13 Clean-finish all of the thread tails using the fray retardant method (see page 18).

14 Use a measuring tape to find the exact center and mark it with pins and a white pencil (photo 10). Apply a small dot of fray retardant to the center and let it dry (photo 11).

15 Cut a ¼-inch (6 mm) square X at the center with a sharp craft knife (photo 12).

16 Push the nipple of the clock workings from the back side of the serged piece through all thicknesses so it comes through to the front side (photo 13).

17 Push the clock's hands onto the nipple to attach them (photo 14).

18 Attach foam-core pieces to each corner of the clock on the back side with white craft glue (photo 15). Attach the clock to the wall with museum wax.

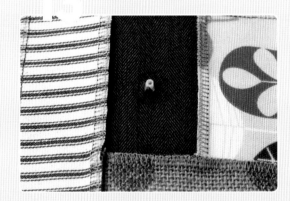

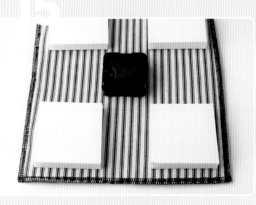

wrap- tie top

Transform a large man's tee into a super sassy and feminine wrap top, with just a few carefully measured cuts and some easy serging.

Gather

- Basic Serging Tool Kit (page 12)
- Man's tee, size large

Serger Setup

(see Preparing Your Serger, page 22)

- Needles: 2
- Stitch width: 6 mm
  - Left needle: Black thread
  - Right needle: Black thread
  - Upper looper: Black thread
  - Lower looper: Black thread

Finished Size:

A man's size large T-shirt was used to make a woman's size small.

Make

1 Lay the tee out flat on your work surface. Measure 6 inches (15.2 cm) down from the top shoulder and mark the center front with a pin.

2 Center 13½ inches (34.3 cm) of the measuring tape across the chest at the top of the tee. Place pins at both ends (photo 1, page 98).

3 Cut out the front neckline, starting at one shoulder, dipping down to the center front pin mark and dipping back up to the opposite shoulder in a symmetric U shape. Cut just below the neck binding along the back.

4 Measure 2 inches (5.1 cm) in from the top neck edge and mark with a white pencil. Make additional marks from that point down to the armpit, in a smooth and gradual angle. Use scissors to cut along the marks, through both front and back thicknesses (photo 2, page 98). Repeat on the other side.

5 Measure 13 inches (33 cm) down from the bottom center of the front neckline and mark with a pin. Use scissors to cut across horizontally through both thicknesses (photo 3). Set aside the cut bottom band for later use.

Note: Because this shirt had horizontal stripes, just one center front pin was enough to guide this cut. If you are using a shirt without stripes, however, measure from the bottom hem to the center front pin and use that measurement to add additional pin marks to guide a straight cut.

6 Flip the shirt over so the back side is facing you. Starting at the neck edge, measure 14½ inches (36.8 cm) down the center back and pin. Use a white pencil and a ruler to draw a line from this pin to the top of each side seam.

7 Starting from the center-back bottom edge, cut up to the center back pin. Cut along the markings on both sides (photo 4).

8 Cut straight across the back from the top of one side seam to the opposite side seam, cutting out a triangular shape. The angled shapes below the cutout are part of the front of the top and will be tied in the back.

9 To make a new bottom for the back of the shirt, use the bottom band you set aside in step 5. First, cut off the original hem and set it aside for later. Lay the bottom band flat on your work surface with the side seams aligned in the center. Cut along one of the folded edges from top to bottom.

10 Starting at the bottom edge of the cut center back, measure up 3½ inches (8.9 cm) and mark it with a white pencil. From that mark, use a ruler to make additional marks at a slight angle all the way up to the side seam. Cut through both thicknesses with scissors (photo 5). These angled shapes will be part of the back of the top and tied in the front.

11 With wrong sides together, pin the back top to the back bottom along adjoining edges. Serge the right sides together (photo 6).

12 Serge around the entire perimeter of all the ties so that all edges are finished.

13 To make neck trim, measure the neckline. From the hem you set aside in step 9, cut a piece to measure slightly less than the neckline. Single-needle-stitch the two short edges with a ¼-inch (6 mm) seam allowance to create the center back of a continuous loop. Fold the loop with the seam on one end and mark the opposite end.

14 Pin the seam of the neck trim loop to the center back of the neckline, wrong sides together. Pin the opposite marked end of the loop to the center front of the neckline. Pin along the back portion of the neckline so that the neck trim lays flat. As you pin toward the center front, there will be some fullness in the top; ease that into the front portion of the neck trim. Single-needle-stitch the trim to the neckline.

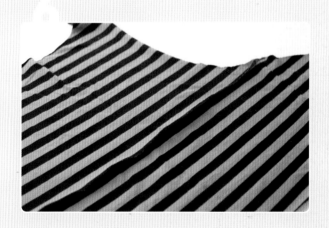

15 Serge along the basted neck edge.

16 Clean-finish all serged thread tails using the large-eye needle method (page 18).

17 Pull the shirt neck over your head, and then wrap the ties on the front of the shirt to the back to tie. Wrap the ties on the back of the shirt to the front and tie.

playful puppets

Sew up this pair of puppets, and then dress them in funky serged outfits that bring their personalities to life.

Gather

For the Puppet Bodies

- Basic Serging Tool Kit (page 12)
- Templates A through J (page 137–138)
- ⅓ yard (30.5 cm) of light brown felt (girl's body parts)
- ⅓ yard (30.5 cm) of dark gray felt (boy's body parts)
- Piece of light blue felt, 5 x 7 inches (12.7 x 17.8 cm) (girl's mouth and front ears)
- Piece of orange felt, 5 x 7 inches (12.7 x 17.8 cm) (boy's mouth and front ears)
- Piece of white felt (eyes)
- Scrap of black felt (shoes)
- Polyester fiberfill
- Pencil or stick
- Black perle cotton

For the Girl Outfit

- Templates K, L, and M (page 138)
- ¼ yard (22.9 cm) of green quilting cotton (dress)
- Piece of orange quilting cotton, 16 x 5 inches (40.6 x 12.7 cm) (apron)
- Piece of blue quilting cotton, 2 x 1¾ inches (5.1 x 4.4 cm) (apron pocket)
- 3 mismatched black buttons

For the Boy Outfit

- Templates N, O, and P (page 138)
- ¼ yard (22.9 cm) black with white dots quilting cotton (vest)
- Piece of taupe with dots quilting cotton, 13 inches (33 cm) square (pants)
- Piece of blue quilting cotton, 2 x 1¾ inches (5.1 x 4.4 cm) (vest pocket)
- Strip of cashmere or other knit fabric, 21 x 1 inches (53.3 x 2.5 cm)
- 3 mismatched brown buttons

Serger Setup

(see Preparing Your Serger, page 22)

- Needles: 1
- Stitch width: 4 mm
  - Right needle: Black thread
  - Upper looper: White thread
  - Lower looper: White thread

Finished Dimensions:

Puppet body: 5 x 10 inches (12.7 x 25.4 cm)

Make

The Puppet Bodies

1 Use the templates to cut the following pieces for each puppet from the appropriate fabric. Transfer all placement marks to the cut pieces as noted on the templates. Double these quantities if you are making both puppets.

- Template A (front body): cut 1
- Template B (back body): cut 1
- Template C (top head): cut 1
- Template D (chin): cut 1
- Template E (arms): cut 2 short and 2 long
- Template F (mouth): cut 1
- Template G (ears): cut 2 front ears and 2 back ears
- Templates H and I (eyes): cut 1 each
- Template J (shoes): cut 2

Project Note Make the puppet body with a single-needle sewing maching, using a ¼-inch (6 mm) seam allowance on all stitching. Use a serger for the puppet clothing.

2 Prepare the ears and arms:

- Stack the short arm pieces and stitch around the perimeter, backstitching at the start and stop points on either side of the straight edge. Repeat for the long arm pieces.
- Pair up the ear fronts with the ear backs and stitch them together in the same way (photo 1).
- Stuff the arms with a tiny bit of fiberfill, leaving approximately the last ½ inch (1.3 cm) of each arm without fiberfill (photo 2).
- Stuff the stitched ears with a tiny bit of fiberfill.

3 Stitch the eyes to the top head per the placement marks (photo 3).

4 Attach the back body parts:

- Align the raw edges of the ears with placement marks on the body back, with the front of the ears facing up. Stitch in place.
- With right sides facing, pin the top head on the back, with the ears in between. Align placement marks at the center of the seam. The top of the head is bigger than the back body edge so you will need to ease the curves as you pin to make everything fit (photo 4).
- Stitch the pieces together.

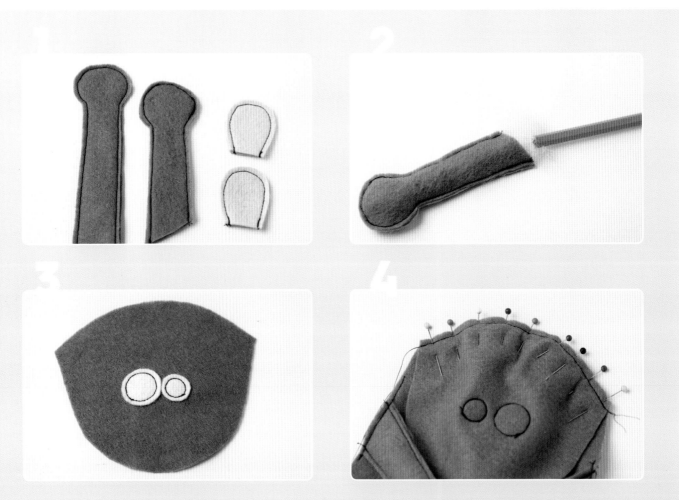

5 Attach the front body parts:

- With right sides facing, stitch the chin to the front body (photo 5).
- Pin the arms to the right side of the front body per the placement marks and stitch in place (photo 6).

6 Attach the mouth:

- With right sides facing, pin the chin to the mouth at the placement marks and stitch them together, backstitching at both ends.
- With right sides facing, pin the top head to the other end of the mouth. The head is larger than the mouth, which will cause the inner mouth to cup in. Start by aligning the center placement marks, then ease the edges together to fit. Stitch in place, backstitching at both ends.

7 Stitch the side seams and turn the puppet right side out. Make French knots for the eyes and nose with black perle cotton and a hand-sewing needle (photo 7).

8 Stitch the shoes to the body front at placement marks.

9 Repeat the instructions to make the second puppet.

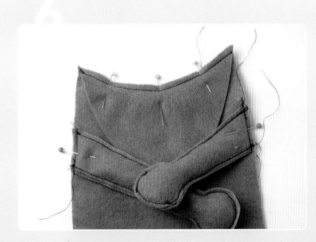

Girl's Outfit

1 Use the templates to cut the following pieces, transferring the pocket placement on template L:

- Template K (dress front and back): cut 2 on fold
- Template L (apron front): cut 1 on fold
- Template M (apron back): cut 1 on fold

2 Make and attach the apron pocket:

- Serge across the bottom and short sides of the blue apron pocket. Fold under the top edge by ½ inch (1.3 cm) (photo 8).
- Tuck in the serged tails and pin the pocket to the apron front at the placement marks, and single-needle-stitch (photo 9).

- Place the front onto the back and serge the side seams (photo 10).

3 Sew the apron:

- With right sides of apron front and back together, serge the two side seams (photo 10).
- Turn the apron right side out and serge the bottom edge, both armholes, and the front and back top edge (photo 11).
- Clean-finish all serged thread tails using the fray-retardant method (page 18).

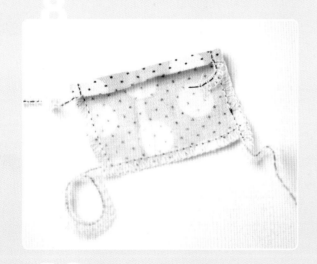

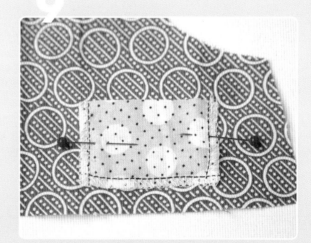

4 Sew the dress:

- For both the front and the back, serge the armholes, then serge across the top neck and bottom edge.
- With right sides of dress front and dress back together, single-needle-stitch the shoulder seams, then the side seams. Clean-finish all serged thread tails using the fray-retardant method (page 18). Turn right side out.

5 Slip the apron over the dress. Secure the apron to the dress by sewing the two buttons on the front (photo 12) and one button on the back, using black thread and a hand-sewing needle. Slip the entire piece onto the puppet.

Boy's Outfit

6 Use the templates to cut out the following pieces, transferring the placement marks on templates N and P:

- Template N (vest front): cut 2
- Template O (vest back): cut 1 on fold
- Template P (pants): cut 2

7 Serge all four sides of the two pieces for the pants (photo 13).

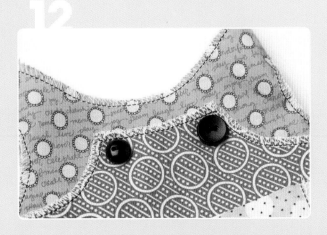

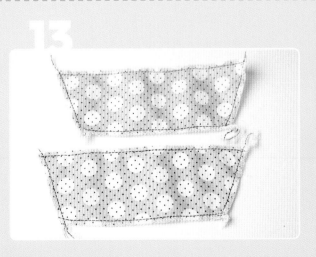

8 Serge all sides and curves (except the shoulders and side seams) of the front and back vest pieces.

9 Follow the Girl's Outfit step 2 instructions for making and attaching the pocket.

10 Complete the outfit:
- With right sides of the vest pieces together, serge the shoulder seams and the side seams (photo 14). Turn right side out and clean-finish all serged threads using the fray-retardant method.
- With both vest and pants right side down, pin the pants to the lower edge of the vest with the pants overlapping the vest edge by approximately ¼ inch (6 mm). Match placement marks with the side seams and the two pants pieces will overlap each other at the center back by approximately ½ inch (1.3 cm) (photo 15).
- Turn the pinned piece over and single-needle-stitch from the right side along the top edge of the serging on the lower vest.
- Clean-finish all serged thread tails using the fray-retardant method.

11 Slip the outfit onto the boy puppet. The vest should overlap itself in front by approximately 1¼ inches (3.2 cm). Pin the overlap in place and slip the vest/pants off the puppet. Hand-sew the three buttons with black thread through both fabric layers (photo 16). Slip the clothing back onto the puppet.

12 Serge around all edges of the cashmere strip and clean-finish all serged thread tails using the fray-retardant method. Wrap the cashmere "scarf" around the puppet's neck area.

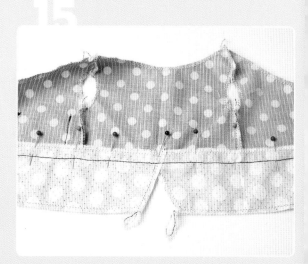

groovy ring belt

Just a few plastic shower curtain rings are all you need to make this groovy belt. Because the rings open and shut easily, you can change out the serged pieces to coordinate with different outfits.

Gather

- Basic Serging Tool Kit (page 12)
- 3 pieces of brown striped fabric (for ring covers), 2 x 10 inches (2.5 x 25.4 cm) each
- ¼ yard (22.9 cm) of brown fabric cut into the following pieces:

- 3 long belt ties, 1½ x 44 inches (3.8 x 112 cm) each
- 2 short connecting strips, 1½ x 4 inches (3.8 x10.2 cm) each
- 3 plastic shower curtain rings, 2⅜ inches (6 cm) in diameter and 7½ inches (19 cm) in circumference

Serger Setup

(see Preparing Your Serger, page 22)

- Needles: 2
- Stitch width: 6 mm
  - Left needle: Tan thread
  - Right needle: Black thread
  - Upper looper: Black thread
  - Lower looper: Brown thread

Finished Size:

52 inches (132 cm) long (including rings and straps)

Make

1 With wrong sides facing, serge together the long edges fabric strips. Do the same with the brown fabric strips: 3 long pieces for the belt ties and 2 short pieces for connecting strips (photo 1).

2 Clean-finish the serged thread tails using the fray retardant method (page 18), making sure that you don't accidentally apply it to the fabric ends.

3 Push an open plastic ring through a serged fabric scrap. Do not close the ring at this point. Repeat for all rings (photo 2).

4 Single-needle-stitch the short ends of a connecting strip together with a ⅜-inch (9.5 mm) seam allowance to create a loop. Repeat for the second connecting strip. Flip the seam allowance to the inside of the loop.

5 Connect two covered rings with a connecting strip/loop by sliding the open rings through. Snap the rings closed. Repeat with the third ring and the remaining connecting strip/loop (photo 3).

6 Stack the three long serged belt ties and loop them through one of the end rings, overlapping by 1½ inches (3.8 cm) (photo 4). Single-needle-stitch the ties in place with a ⅜-inch (9.5 mm) seam allowance.

7 Clean-finish all serged thread tails hanging on the edges of the belt ties using the fray retardant method.

Tip Gather fabrics and fabric scraps in different colors and prepare sets of serged strips. Any time you want to change out the colors of the belt, pop open the plastic rings and swap the ring covers, connecting strips, and ties and then snap the rings back in place.

long and sleek skirt

This skirt is designed with jersey knits that have enough give and pull to make the final garment a singular size that fits most women.

Gather

- Basic Serging Tool Kit (page 12)
- Template A (page 139)
- 1 yard (.9 m) of gray single-knit jersey, 60 inches (152.4 cm) wide
- Four coordinating tees, all in Men's size large

Serger Setup

(see **Preparing Your Serger,** page 22) Needles: 1
- Stitch width: 4 mm
  - Right needle: Black thread
  - Upper looper: Black thread
  - Lower looper: Black thread

Finished Size:

28 inches (71.1 cm) around the waist x 35 inches (88.9 cm) long

Make

1 Cut the jersey into the following pieces:
- 1 piece for the upper skirt: 33 x 18½ inches (83.8 x 47 cm)
- 2 pieces for the waistband: each 14 x 8½ inches (35.6 x 21.6 cm)

2 With template A, cut nine pieces from the assorted T-shirts and two pieces from the gray jersey.

3 Refer to the diagram (right) and cut the jersey upper skirt into three pieces: one trapezoid, one triangle, and one irregular pentagon. Then serge the cut pieces back together, wrong sides facing: Start by serging the small triangle to the pentagon, then serge this joined piece to the trapezoid.

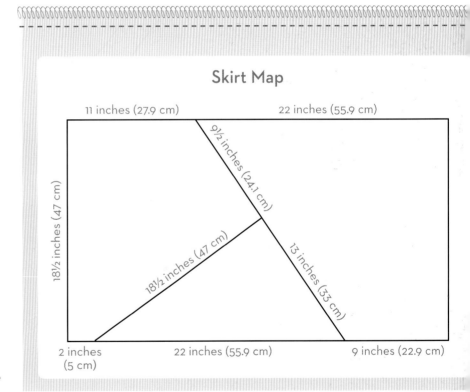

Skirt Map

4 Pin two of the nine template A pieces with wrong sides facing, and serge along one long side. Open up this piece and freehand cut diagonally across the middle (photo 1). Then serge the cut pieces back together, wrong sides facing (photo 2).

5 Repeat step 4 four more times, freehand cutting diagonals at different lengths, angles, and directions. You will have four joined pieces and one single piece from template A. Cut this single piece in the middle diagonally and then serge those pieces back together.

6 With wrong sides facing, serge the long sides of the pieces from steps 4 and 5 together to make the lower portion of the skirt (photo 3).

7 With wrong sides facing, pin the top edge of the lower skirt to the bottom edge of the upper skirt. Serge these pieces together (photo 4).

8 With wrong sides together, pin and then serge the center back of the entire skirt.

9 To find the center front, fold the skirt in half with the center back on one side and mark the

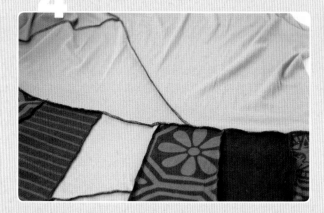

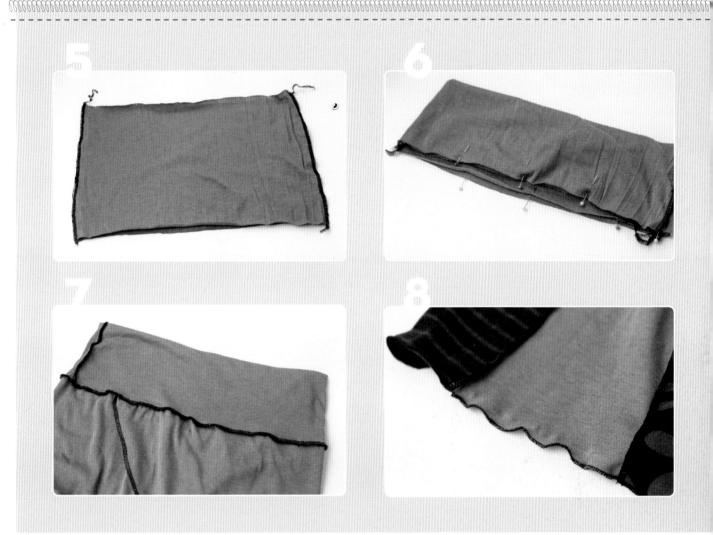

opposite fold on the top (waistband) edge with a water-soluble pen. Now fold the skirt in the opposite direction, matching the front and center backs, and mark the sides.

10 To make the waistband:
- Stack the two waistband pieces with wrong sides together and serge together both short ends to create a waistband ring (photo 5).
- Fold down the top half of the waistband onto itself, matching the raw edges, so that it becomes a double-layered ring (photo 6). Pin and single-needle baste-stitch the raw edges together.
- Measure or fold the waistband to fit the center front and center back. Mark each spot with a pin.

11 To attach the waistband:
- With wrong sides facing, pin the waistband to the top of the skirt, aligning the raw edges. Align serged waistband seams with the skirt side seam marks; match up the center front marks and center back marks. The waistband is smaller than the skirt, so you'll need to stretch the waistband to fit and add lots of pins all the way around.
- Single-needle baste-stitch the waistband to the skirt, and then serge the pieces together (photo 7).

12 Serge the hem. Give the hem a bit of a tug while you serge to get a ruffly look (photo 8).

13 Clean-finish all serged thread tails using the large-eye needle method (page 18).

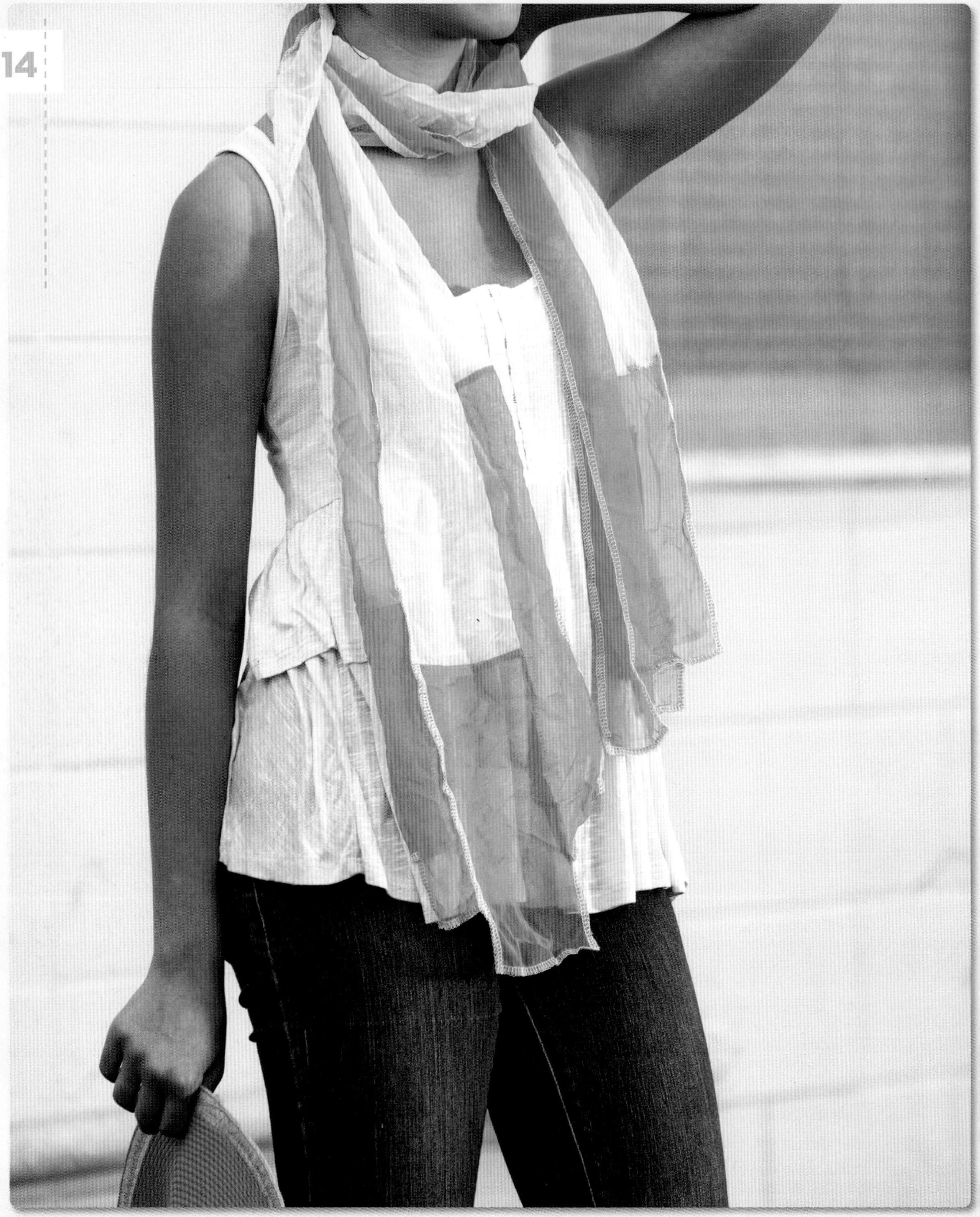

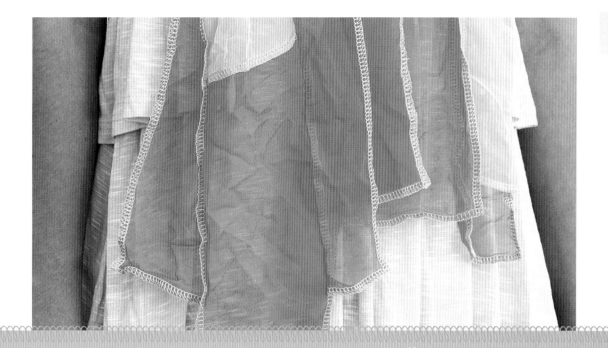

pleated and crinkled scarf

After you measure, rip, cut, and serge this scarf, let it develop crinkly wrinkles by wetting it, heating it, and letting it slowly cool down.

Gather

- Basic Serging Tool Kit (page 12)
- ⅓ yard (30.5 cm) of 58-inch-wide (147.3 cm) orange polyester chiffon
- ⅓ yard (30.5 cm) of 58-inch-wide (147.3 cm) cream polyester chiffon
- Dish towel
- Microwave oven

Serger Setup

(see Preparing Your Serger, page 22)

- Needles: 2
- Stitch width: 6 mm
  - Left needle: Cream thread
  - Right needle: Cream thread
  - Upper looper: Cream thread
  - Lower looper: Cream thread

Finished Dimensions:

75¼ x 12 inches (190.5 x 30.48 cm)

Rip vs. Cut Because it is almost impossible to cut chiffon on the straight of grain, it is better to rip rather than cut long strips so you get a true grainline. The widths for ripping the chiffon into strips are approximations. They could become slightly narrower if the fabric rips slightly askew.

Make

1 From selvage to selvage, rip the orange chiffon into three strips at the widths listed below, and then cut each strip with scissors into smaller pieces (see diagram A):

From a width of 2¼ inches (5.7 cm), cut 3 lengths:
- A: 7¼ inches (18.4 cm)
- B: 9 inches (22.9 cm)
- C: 57 inches (144.8 cm) long

From a width of 3½ inches (8.9 cm), cut 2 lengths:
- D: 14 inches (35.6 cm)
- E: 40 inches (101.6 cm)

From a width of 4 inches (10.2 cm), cut 2 lengths:
- F: 9 inches (22.9 cm)
- G: 9¼ inches (23.5 cm)

2 From selvage to selvage, rip the cream chiffon into three strips at the widths listed below, and then cut each strip with scissors into smaller pieces (see diagram B).

From a width of 2¼ inches (5.7 cm), cut 2 lengths:
- H: 15 inches (38.1 cm)
- I: 57 inches (144.8 cm)

From a width of 3½ inches (8.9 cm), cut 1 length:
- J: 19 inches (48.3 cm)

From a width of 4 inches (10.2 cm), cut 1 length:
- K: 57 inches (144.8 cm)

3 Make scarf strip #1:
- Align the short ends of A and I. Serge them together.
- Align the other short end of I with the short end of B and serge.

4 Make scarf strip #2 by aligning the short ends of C and H and serging.

5 Make scarf strip #3:
- Align the short ends of G and K and serge.
- Align the other short end of J with the short end of E and serge.

6 Make scarf strip #4:
- Align the short ends of D and J and serge.
- Align the other short end of K with the short end of F and serge.

7 Serge all the remaining short ends of all four strips (photo 1).

a

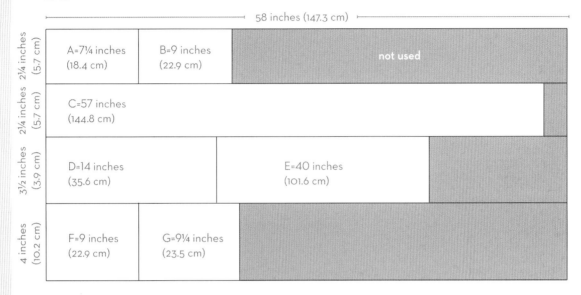

58 inches (147.3 cm)

2¼ inches (5.7 cm)
A=7¼ inches (18.4 cm) | B=9 inches (22.9 cm) | not used

2¼ inches (5.7 cm)
C=57 inches (144.8 cm)

3½ inches (3.9 cm)
D=14 inches (35.6 cm) | E=40 inches (101.6 cm)

4 inches (10.2 cm)
F=9 inches (22.9 cm) | G=9¼ inches (23.5 cm)

b

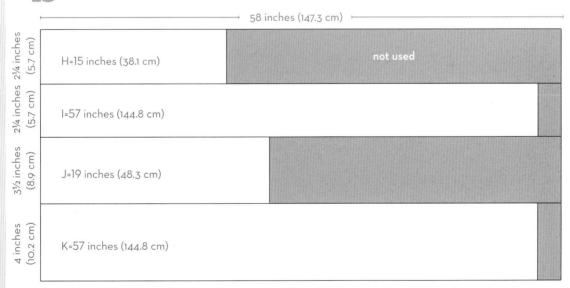

58 inches (147.3 cm)

2¼ inches (5.7 cm)
H=15 inches (38.1 cm) | not used

2¼ inches (5.7 cm)
I=57 inches (144.8 cm)

3½ inches (8.9 cm)
J=19 inches (48.3 cm)

4 inches (10.2 cm)
K=57 inches (144.8 cm)

8 The four scarf strips will have different lengths as follows:

- Scarf strip #1: 73¼ inches (186 cm)
- Scarf strip #2: 72 inches (182.9 cm)
- Scarf strip #3: 75¼ inches (191.1 cm)
- Scarf strip #4: 63 inches (147.3 cm)

Find and mark the centers of each scarf with a pin and lay them horizontally on a flat surface, with #1 on the bottom and #4 on top, with the serged seams facing you. Because they are different lengths, serging them with centers aligned will give the scarf a staggered look (see diagram C).

9 Assemble the scarf:

- With wrong sides together, pin strips #1 and #2 along the long edges with centers aligned and serge. Make sure that you push the short-end seams in the same direction as you are serging the long edges.

- With right sides together, pin this piece to strip #3 along the long edges with centers aligned and serge.
- With wrong sides together, pin this piece to strip #4 along the long edges with centers aligned and serge.

10 Clean finish all serged thread tails by using the large-eye needle method (see page 18).

11 Wet the scarf, crinkle it into a ball, wrap it into the dish towel, and microwave it on high for a minute. At the end of the minute, check the scarf; it will be steamy and hot. Crinkle it back up into a ball, wrap it in the dish towel, and microwave it on high for another minute. Let it cool while it is still wadded up in a ball and then remove it from the dish towel; you will find a scarf that is nice and crinkly. If the scarf is still damp, drape it over a hanger until it is completely dry.

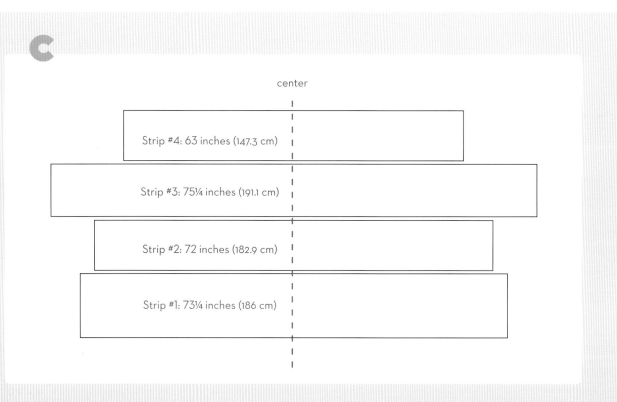

C

center

Strip #4: 63 inches (147.3 cm)

Strip #3: 75¼ inches (191.1 cm)

Strip #2: 72 inches (182.9 cm)

Strip #1: 73¼ inches (186 cm)

jellyfish
under the sea

This jellyfish project has a solid body and tentacles with lots of movement. It's a terrific decorative piece for anyone who loves sea creatures.

Gather

- Basic Serging Tool Kit (page 12)
- Templates A and B (page 134)
- 6 pieces of cotton fabric in assorted blues and greens, 6 x 8 inches (15.2 x 20.3 cm)
- 1 piece of cotton fabric in blue or green, 10 inches (25.4 cm) square
- Orange fabric scrap, approximately 5 inches (12.7 cm) square
- Paper-backed fusible web (slightly larger than orange fabric scrap)
- Quarter and dime
- Pencil
- Teal perle cotton
- Strips of chiffon and jersey knit, ½ to 2 inches (1.3 to 5.1 cm) wide:
  - 2 blue jersey knit wavy strips, 28 inches (71.1 cm) long*
  - 1 blue jersey knit wavy strip, 22 inches (55.9 cm) long*
  - 6 cream chiffon strips, each 18 inches (45.7 cm) long
  - 6 aqua chiffon strips, each 30 inches (76.2 cm) long
  - 4 orange chiffon strips, each 30 inches (76.2 cm) long
- Polyester fiberfill, approximately 3 ounces (85 gr)

* *To make the jersey strips look wavy when serged, cut the long edges in a wavy line, not a straight one (see step 4).*

Serger Setup

(see Preparing Your Serger, page 22)

- Needles: 1
- Stitch width: 6 mm
  - Left needle: Black thread
  - Upper looper: Black thread
  - Lower looper: Black thread

Finished Dimensions:

8 x 38 inches (20.3 x 96.5 cm)

Make

1 Use the templates to cut the following pieces:
- Template A (from assorted blues and greens): cut 6
- Template B (from blue or green square): cut 1

2 Make the jellyfish sides:
- With wrong sides together, serge two A pieces along one of the long curved sides. Serge a third side piece to this piece in the same manner. You now have what looks like the top of half an umbrella.
- Repeat step with the other three side pieces (photo 1).

- With wrong sides together, serge the two half umbrella top pieces all around the top curve (photo 2).

3 Make the orange spots:
- Following the manufacturer's instructions, fuse paper-backed fusible web onto the orange fabric scrap.
- Trace 6 circles using a quarter as the template, and 11 circles using a dime as the template.
- Cut out the traced circles and peel off the paper backing.

- Fuse the circles onto the lower portion of the serged jellyfish body. Space them so that one large and two small circles fit in each of the six serged segments.
- Overcast stitch all of the fused circles with teal perle cotton and a hand-sewing needle (photo 3).

4 Make the jersey tentacles:
- Round off one of the ends of a blue jersey knit strip and cut it to a point (photo 4).
- Serge one of the long wavy edges, making sure that you pull the fabric a little bit while you are serging to get an exaggerated wavy look. Repeat on the other long wavy edge (photo 5).

- Repeat for the remaining two jersey strips.

5 Attach the tentacles:
- Fold under the top edge of each jersey tentacle and pin them to the jellyfish bottom (B) as shown, spaced evenly apart about 1 inch (2.5 cm) from the outer edge of the circle (photo 6). Topstitch in place.
- Attach the six cream chiffon strips in the same way, evenly spaced around the edge, slightly closer to the edge than the jersey strips (photo 7). Make sure to leave room for the seam allowance you'll need for B. Topstitch in place.
- Attach the six aqua chiffon strips closer to the center than the jersey tentacles (photo 8).

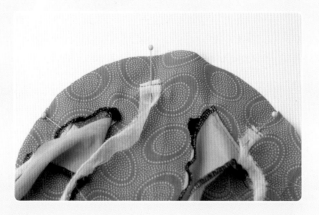

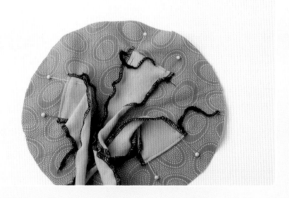

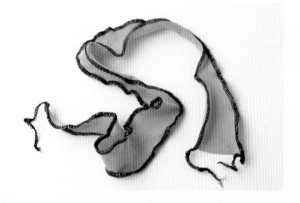

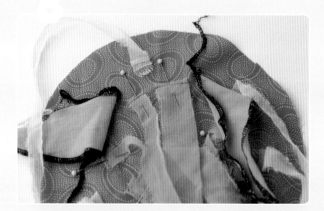

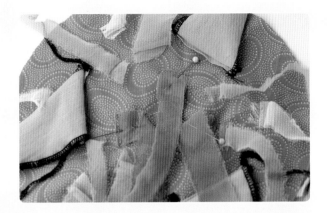

- Finish by attaching the orange chiffon strips in the center (photo 9).

6 Assemble the jellyfish:
- Stuff the body of the jellyfish with fiberfill (photo 10).
- Generously pin the top and bottom portions of the jellyfish together and baste (photo 11). Remove the pins.
- Serge around the outer edge of the jellyfish (photo 12).

7 Make the hanger:
- With a hand-sewing needle and thread, pierce the top of the jellyfish and push the needle all the way through and out the bottom.
- Make one straight stitch across and push the needle back through the top. Secure with a knot. This will keep the bottom base nipped up to the top and stabilize it.
- Create a loop with the thread at the top as the holder.

retro chic apron

This apron is filled with details galore: rounded corners, double fabric layers, and a touch of cashmere accents. It's so cute, you'll want to wear it in the kitchen and elsewhere, as a fashion accessory.

Gather

- Basic Serging Tool Kit (page 12)
- ⅔ yard (61 cm) polyester suiting (underlayer)
- ½ yard (45.7 cm) of quilting cotton (top layer)
- 1 upcycled cashmere sweater (belt and trim)
- Small plastic lid or cap
- 16 inches (40.6 cm) of double-fold bias tape (cream)
- Perle cotton (pink)

Serger Setup

(see Preparing Your Serger, page 22) Needles: 1
- Stitch width: 4 mm
  - Right needle: Black thread
  - Upper looper: Gray thread
  - Lower looper: Pink thread

Finished Size:

28 x 19½ inches (71.1 x 49.5 cm)

Make

1 From the polyester suiting, cut the following pieces:
- For the underlayer, a piece measuring 28 x 18 inches (71.1 x 45.7 cm)
- For the pocket, a 9½-inch (24.1 cm) square

2 From the quilting cotton, cut a piece that measures 20 x 15 inches (50.8 x 38.1 cm).

3 From the upcycled sweater:
- Cut one of the side seams of the sweater's waistband hem and then carefully cut into the sweater to make a 36 x 2¼-inch (91.4 x 5.7 cm) strip (see Sweater Note on next page). Leave the other side seam intact; it will become the center front for the apron.
- Also cut a 12 x 1½-inch (30.5 x 3.8 cm) strip from the body of the sweater for the pocket trim.

The waistband for this apron was made from the 2¼-inch (5.7 cm) hem of a cashmere sweater, with the finished side becoming the top edge of the waistband. If your sweater doesn't have a wide enough hem, cut a strip along the hem that is 2¼ inches (5.7 cm) wide.

4 Fold the quilting cotton top layer in half, widthwise. Place a small plastic lid or cap onto the bottom nonfolded corner and trace the curve of the lid to round off the corners (photo 1). Cut along the traced mark through both thicknesses (photo 2). Repeat with the underlayer (photo 2).

5 With the right side facing up, serge around the left side, bottom, and right side of the top layer. Press with an iron. Repeat with the underlayer (photo 3).

6 Make the pocket:
- With the right side facing up, fold the pocket piece 1¼ inches (3.2 cm) from the left-hand side and press. Serge along the fold without cutting into the fabric (photo 4).
- Fold and press the pocket again 1 inch (2.5 cm) from the serged fold. Serge along the new fold. Repeat this step five more times for a total of seven serged ridges.
- With the right side facing up and all serged ridges facing in the same direction, serge the top edge of the pocket piece.
- Fold over the top serged edge to the right side by 1¼ inches (3.2 cm) and pin. Single-needle-stitch ¼ inch (6 mm) from each side, from the top folded edge to the bottom of the folded edge, backstitching at both ends (photo 5).
- Clip the corners at a diagonal, turn the hemmed pocket top to the inside, and press the top folded edge. Press under the two side edges and bottom edge by ¼ inch (6 mm).
- Single-needle-stitch the folded top edge, 1 inch (2.5 cm) down from the fold.

7 Add the pocket trim:

- Serge the two long sides of the cashmere pocket trim strip.
- Fold under one of the short sides of the cashmere trim by ½ inch (1.3 cm) and place it on top of the pocket piece, approximately ¼ inch (6 mm) from the top edge. Make three French knots through all thicknesses, using a hand-sewing needle and pink perle cotton.
- Pinch and fold the cashmere trim by approximately ½ inch (6 mm) to make a ridge. Make three French knots through all thicknesses.
- Repeat seven more times, with the final three French knots made close to the right edge of the pocket (photo 6).

8 Single-needle-stitch the pocket onto the top layer, 3½ inches (8.9 cm) down from the top edge and 3 inches (7.6 cm) in from the side edge (photo 7).

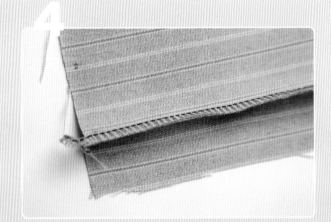

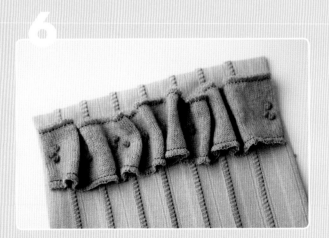

9 Assemble and gather the layers:

- With center fronts matching, stack the top layer on the underlayer.

- Make two rows of basting stitches starting 2 inches (5.1 cm) to the left of the center front, making sure to backstitch at the start only of both rows (photo 8). Repeat for the right side.

- Pull the threads on the side to gather the center front to each side edge to a length of approximately 7½ inches (19 cm). Evenly distribute the gathers.

- With right sides facing, place the long edge of the double-fold bias tape onto the gathered left side of the apron and pin, allowing approximately ½ inch (6 mm) of the bias tape to extend beyond the apron (photo 9). Repeat for the right side.

- Single-needle-stitch through all thicknesses (photo 10).

- Fold the ½-inch (6 mm) bias-tape extension in toward the gathering, fold it over the bias tape, and zigzag stitch through all thicknesses, from one side to the other side of the apron.

10 Make and attach the waistband:

- Serge one short side, the long side with raw edges, and other short side of the waistband strip.

- Clean-finish the serged thread tails using the large-eye needle method (page 18).

- With center fronts matching, pin the cashmere strip on top of the apron, covering the bias tape. Single-needle-stitch in place (photo 11).

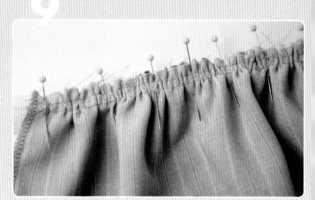

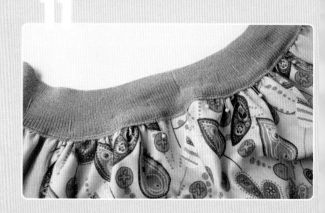

wired flowers wreath

Make a bold and lovely statement in your entryway, or any other room in the house, with this wreath adorned with fabric flowers.

Gather

- Basic Serging Tool Kit (page 12)
- Templates A, B, and C (page 134)
- ¼ yard (22.9 cm) of natural-colored linen
- Scraps of quilting cotton in assorted aquas
- Scraps of brown felt
- 12 feet (10 m) of 28-gauge wire, cut into:
  - six 16-inch (40.6 cm) lengths
  - six 13-inch (33 cm) lengths
- Hot glue gun and glue sticks
- Grapevine wreath, 12 inches (30.5 cm) in diameter

Serger Setup

(see Preparing Your Serger, page 22)

- Needles: 1
- Stitch width: 4 mm
  - Right needle: Tan thread
  - Upper looper: Cream thread
  - Lower looper: Cream thread

Finished Dimensions:

Large linen flower: 10 inches (25.4 cm) in diameter

Make

1 Use the templates to cut the following flower pieces:

- Template A: cut 6 petals from linen
- Template B: cut 12 petals from assorted aqua scraps (6 fronts and 6 backs)
- Template C: cut 3 pieces from brown felt

2 Prepare each linen flower petal:

- Serge around outer edges of all six linen petals (photo 1).

- Thread the large-eye needle with one of the longer wires and pull it through the serged edge on the back side of the petal (photo 2).
- At the point, pull the needle out of the serged edge and then push it back in, so you can make it around the curve (photo 3).
- Clean-finish the serged threads using fray-retardant method (page 18).
- Twist the ends of the wire together several times, pulling slightly so that the fabric "cups" a bit (photo 4).

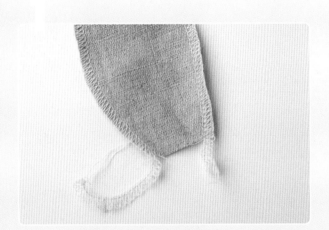

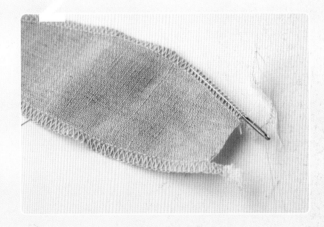

3 Assemble the linen petals:
- Grab two linen petals and twist their wires together (photo 5).
- Do the same with the remaining petals, one at a time.
- Curl, bend, and shape the petals as desired. Twist and flatten all the wires so that they can remain hidden behind the flower (photo 6).

4 Twist the wires of the flower around some of the vines and then hot glue gun the flower to the wreath.

5 Make the petals for the aqua flowers:
- With wrong sides together, serge two of the aqua petals along the outer edge. Stitch pairs together until you have 6 petals.
- Thread the large-eye needle with one of the shorter wires and pull it through the serged edge on the back side of each petal (photo 7).
- Clean-finish all serged thread tails using the fray-retardant method.
- With a hand-sewing needle and aqua thread, make large running stitches on the inside curve of each petal (photo 8).

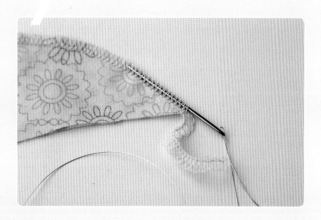

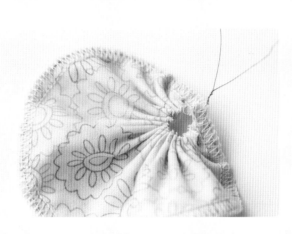

8 Finish the aqua flowers by attaching the brown felt centers with a hot glue gun.

9 Hot glue the aqua blooms to the wreath, one in the center of the linen flower, and the other one on each side.

- Draw up the thread and knot it, then twist the wires together (photo 9).
- Overlap the curved ends to shape the flower (photo 10). There is no need to hot-glue or stitch the bloom because the wire holds the shape.

6 Stack two of the serged aqua blooms and stitch them together (photo 11). Stitch the remaining pairs and set them aside.

7 Make three brown flower centers:
- With a hand-sewing needle and brown thread, make a large running stitch along the curved edge of one of the felt pieces (photo 12).
- Pull the thread to gather the edge.
- Curl the ends around to form the center and stitch to secure (photo 13).

templates

Under the Sea Jellyfish
page 119
enlarge 200%

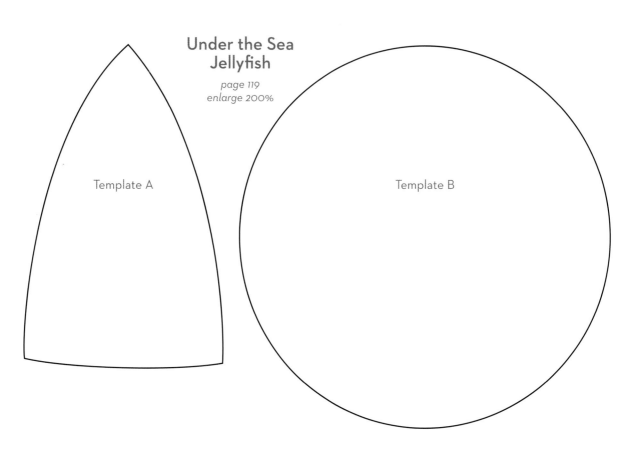

Template A

Template B

Wired Flowers Wreath
page 129
enlarge 200%

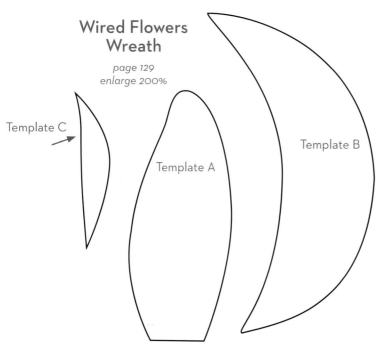

Template C

Template A

Template B

Ombré-Hexagon Burp Cloth
page 78
enlarge 200%

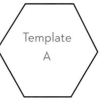

Template A

Template B

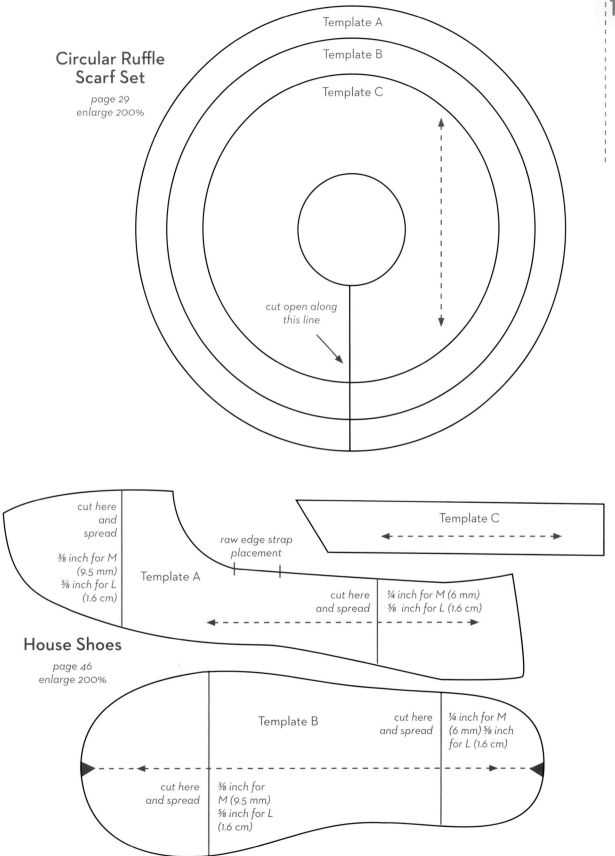

Circular Ruffle Scarf Set

page 29
enlarge 200%

Template A

Template B

Template C

cut open along this line

House Shoes

page 46
enlarge 200%

cut here and spread

⅜ inch for M (9.5 mm)
⅝ inch for L (1.6 cm)

Template A

raw edge strap placement

Template C

cut here and spread

¼ inch for M (6 mm)
⅝ inch for L (1.6 cm)

cut here and spread

Template B

cut here and spread

¼ inch for M (6 mm) ⅝ inch for L (1.6 cm)

cut here and spread

⅜ inch for M (9.5 mm)
⅝ inch for L (1.6 cm)

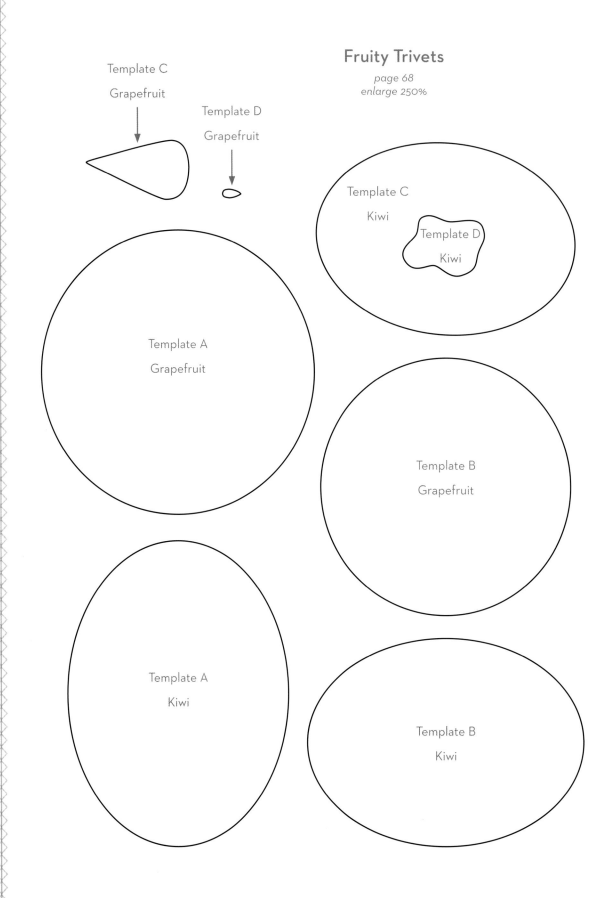

Fruity Trivets

page 68
enlarge 250%

Template C
Grapefruit

Template D
Grapefruit

Template C
Kiwi

Template D
Kiwi

Template A
Grapefruit

Template B
Grapefruit

Template A
Kiwi

Template B
Kiwi

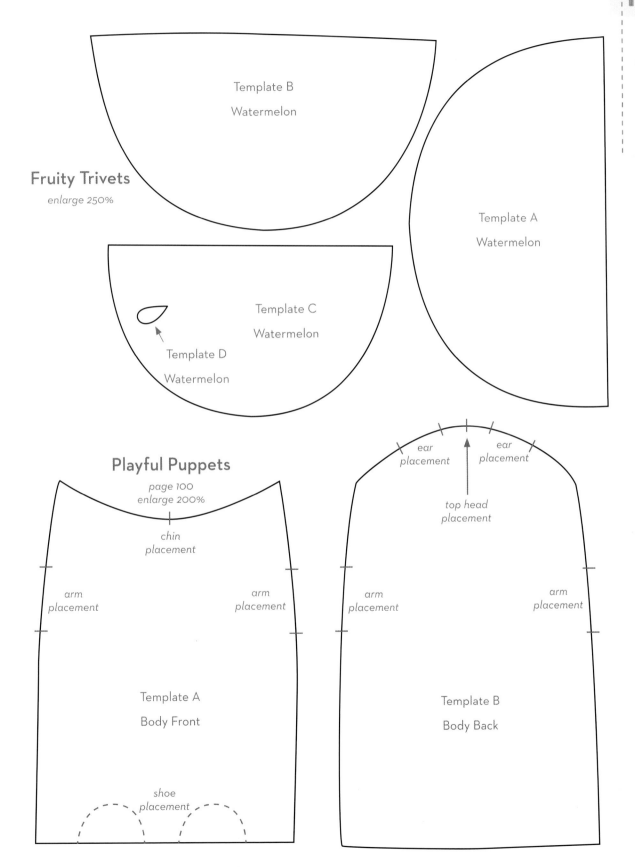

Fruity Trivets

enlarge 250%

Template B
Watermelon

Template A
Watermelon

Template C
Watermelon

Template D
Watermelon

Playful Puppets

*page 100
enlarge 200%*

chin placement

arm placement

arm placement

Template A
Body Front

shoe placement

ear placement

top head placement

ear placement

arm placement

arm placement

Template B
Body Back

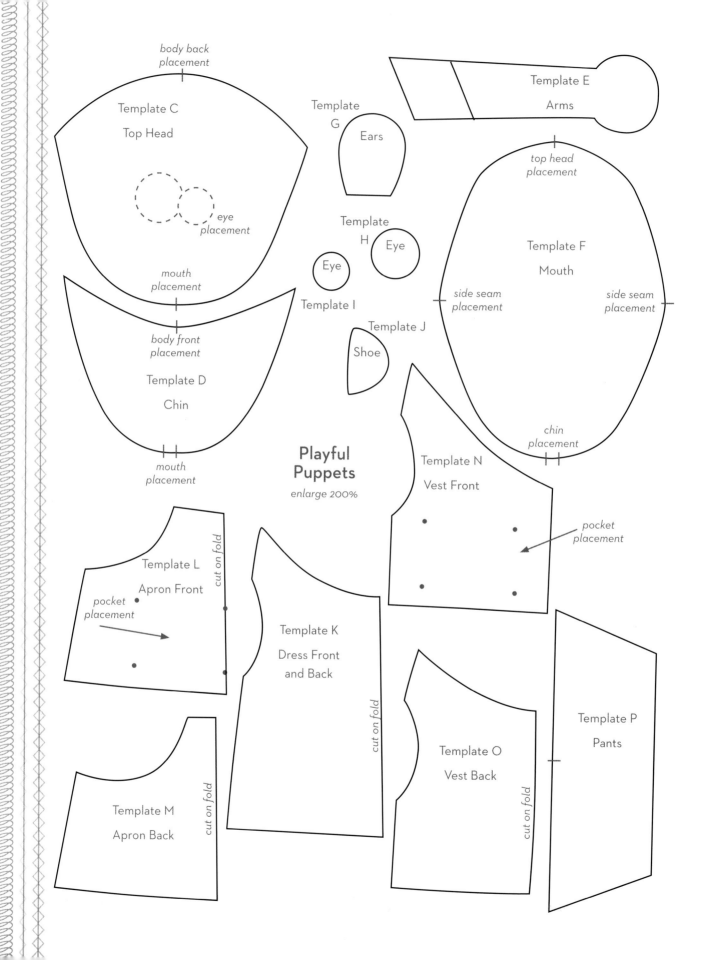

Template C

Top Head

body back placement

eye placement

mouth placement

body front placement

Template D

Chin

mouth placement

Template G

Ears

Template H

Eye

Eye

Template I

Template J

Shoe

Playful Puppets

enlarge 200%

Template E

Arms

top head placement

Template F

Mouth

side seam placement

side seam placement

chin placement

Template N

Vest Front

pocket placement

Template L

Apron Front

pocket placement

cut on fold

Template K

Dress Front and Back

cut on fold

Template M

Apron Back

cut on fold

Template O

Vest Back

cut on fold

Template P

Pants

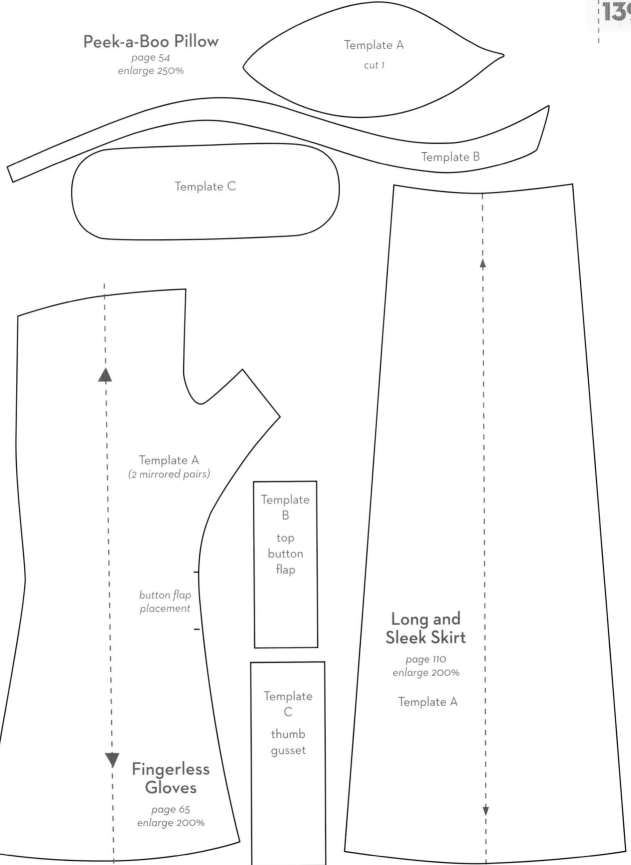

Peek-a-Boo Pillow
page 54
enlarge 250%

Template A
cut 1

Template B

Template C

Template A
(2 mirrored pairs)

button flap placement

Template B
top button flap

Template C
thumb gusset

Fingerless Gloves
page 65
enlarge 200%

Long and Sleek Skirt
page 110
enlarge 200%

Template A

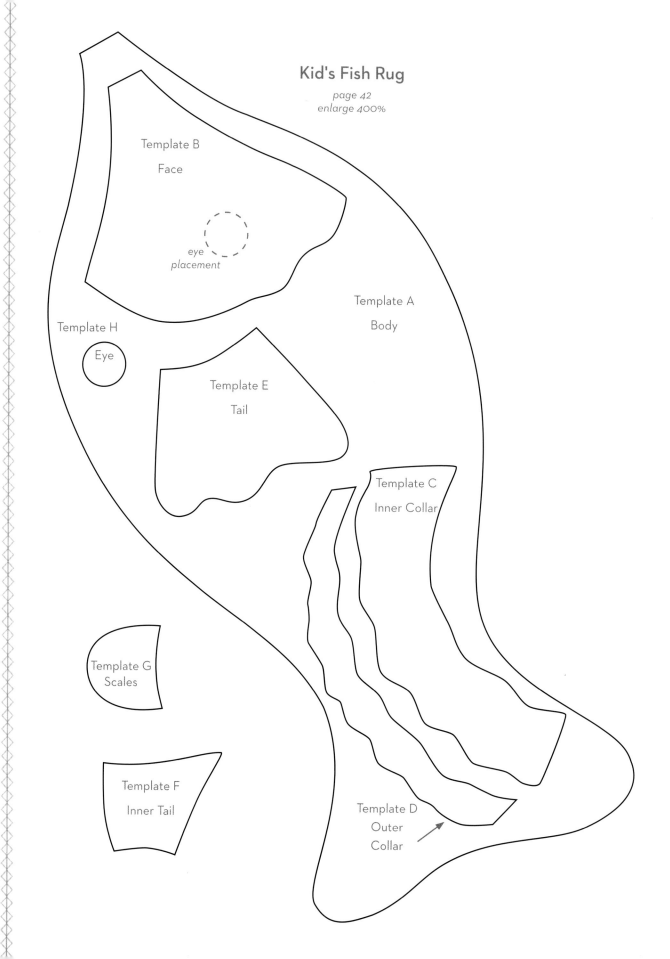

Kid's Fish Rug

page 42
enlarge 400%

Template B

Face

eye
placement

Template A

Body

Template H

Eye

Template E

Tail

Template C

Inner Collar

Template G
Scales

Template F

Inner Tail

Template D

Outer
Collar

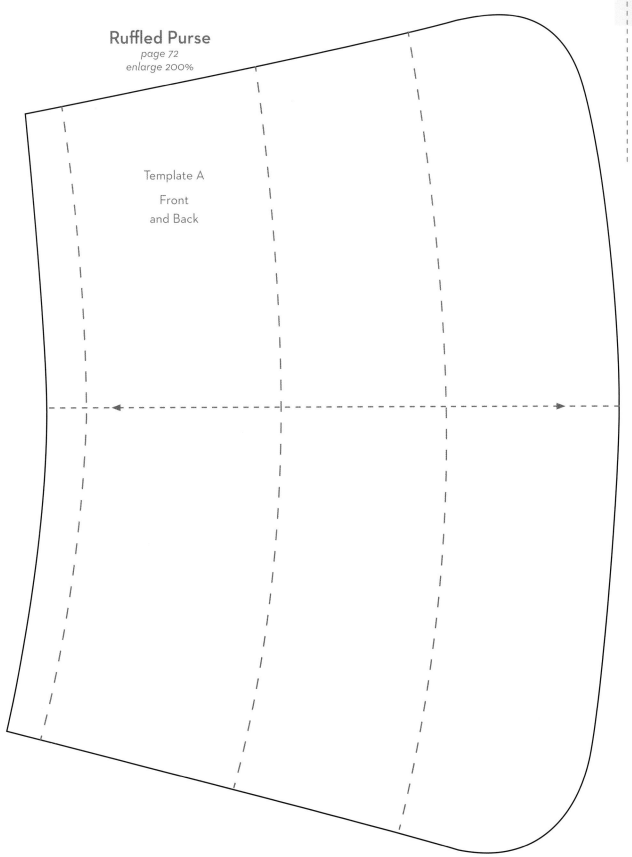

Ruffled Purse
page 72
enlarge 200%

Template A

Front
and Back

13 inches (33 cm)

Child's Bloomers

page 32
enlarge 225%

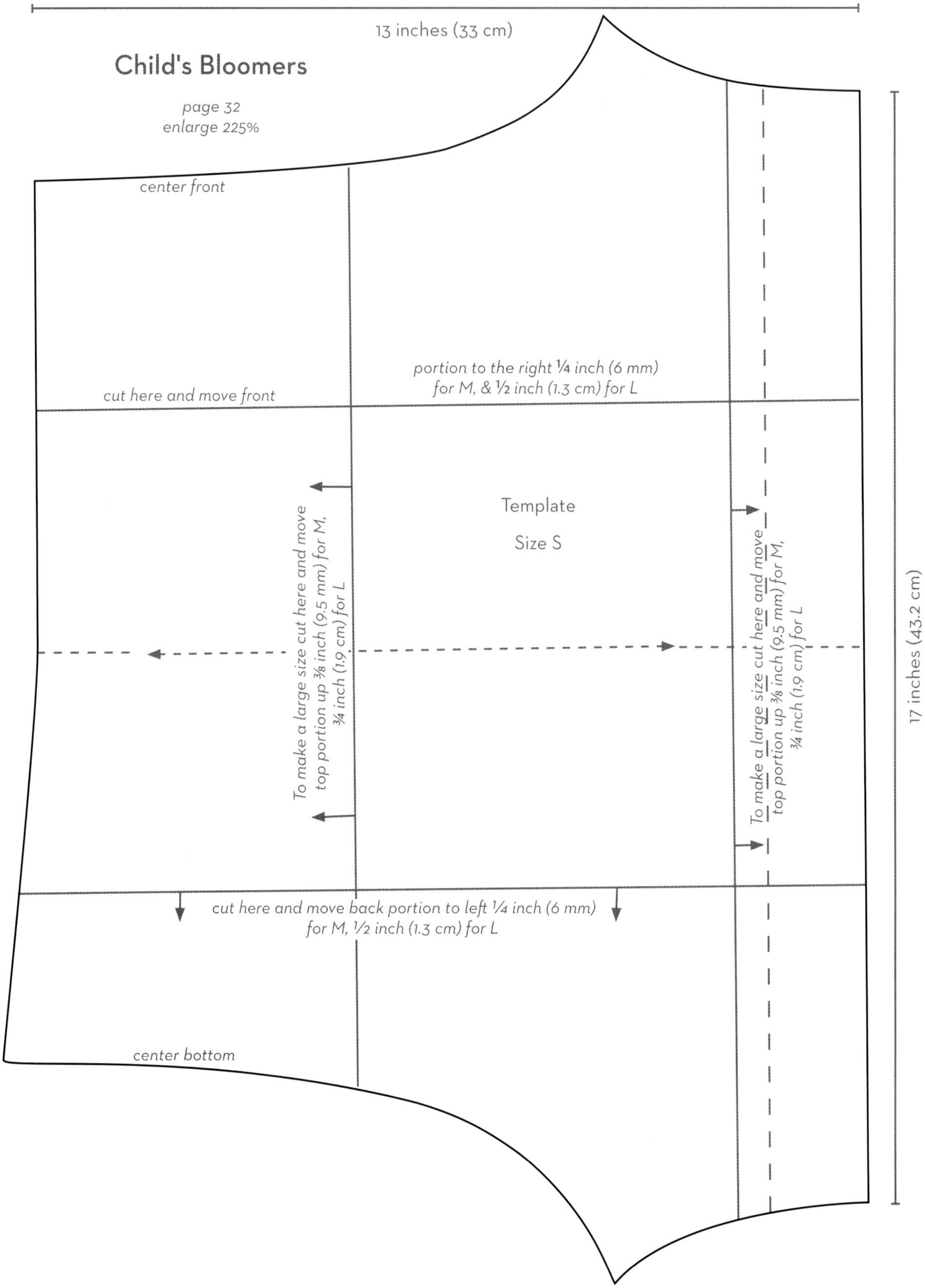

center front

cut here and move front

portion to the right ¼ inch (6 mm)
for M, & ½ inch (1.3 cm) for L

Template

Size S

To make a large size cut here and move
top portion up ⅜ inch (9.5 mm) for M,
¾ inch (1.9 cm) for L

To make a large size cut here and move
top portion up ⅜ inch (9.5 mm) for M,
¾ inch (1.9 cm) for L

cut here and move back portion to left ¼ inch (6 mm)
for M, ½ inch (1.3 cm) for L

center bottom

17 inches (43.2 cm)

about the authors

Jenny Doh is head of *www.crescendoh.com*. She has authored and packaged numerous books including *Crochet Love*, *Craft-a-Doodle*, *Print Collective*, *Creative Lettering*, *Stamp It!*, *Journal It!*, *We Make Dolls!*, *Hand in Hand*, and *Signature Styles*. She lives in Santa Ana, California, and loves to create, stay fit, and play music.

Cynthia Shaffer is a mixed-media artist, quilter, and creative sewer. She is the author of *Stash Happy: Patchwork*, and *Stash Happy: Appliqué*. Cynthia lives in Orange, California, with her husband, Scott; her sons, Corry and Cameron; and their beloved Boston Terriers. Visit *www.cynthiashaffer.com*.

resources

Serger and Sewing Machine Information

If you're in the market for a serger and not finding what you need locally, check out the websites below. There are also numerous helpful videos at www.youtube.com, including how to thread a serger.

http://babylock.com/sergers
www.bernina.com
www.brother-usa.com
http://content.janome.com/index.cfm/
  Machines/Sergers
www.jukihome.com/products/
  sergingmain.html
www.sears.com
www.singerco.com/products/
  category/sergers

index

Editor: **Amanda Carestio**
Art Director: **Shannon Yokeley**
Graphic Designer: **Raquel Joya**
Cover Designer: **Elizabeth Mihaltse**
Technical Editor: **Kathy P. Brock**
Copyeditors: **Nancy D. Wood,**
    Amanda Crabtree Weston

Photographer: **Cynthia Shaffer**
Project Designer: **Cynthia Shaffer**
Assistant Editors: **Monica Mouet,**
    Kerri Winterstein
Models: **Cara Calise, Jennifer Furry,**
    Sierra Reynolds, Cameron Shaffer